MARCO ⊕ POLO

M000159286

NEW ZEA LAND

PAPUA SOLOM.
NEW GUINEA
Coral Sea VANUATU
FIJI
New Caledonia (FR.)
PAZIFIC OCEAN
AUSTRALIA ○ Brisbane
NEW ZEALAND
Canberra ○ Sydney
○
Melbourne
Tasman Sea ○ Wellington
Chatham Islands (NZ)
Tasmania

www.marco-polo.com

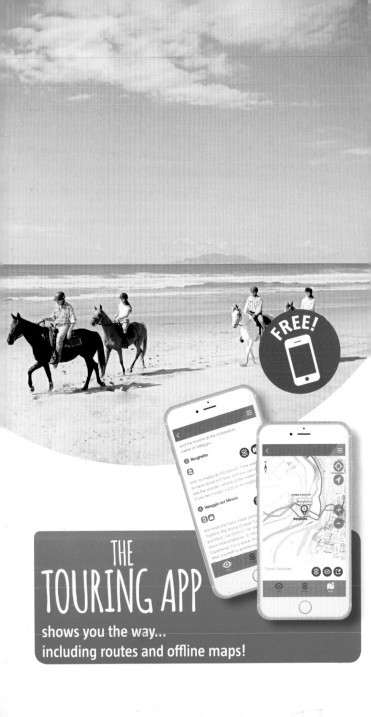

FREE!

THE
TOURING APP

shows you the way...
including routes and offline maps!

GET MORE OUT OF YOUR MARCO POLO GUIDE

IT'S AS SIMPLE AS THIS

1 go.marco-polo.com/nzl

2 download and discover

GO!

WORKS OFFLINE!

SYMBOLS

INSIDER TIP ▶ Insider Tip

★ Highlight

●●●● Best of ...

🌿 Scenic view

🌍 Responsible travel: fair
trade principles and the
environment respected

(*) Telephone numbers
that are not toll-free

PRICE CATEGORIES HOTELS

Expensive over NZ\$235

Moderate NZ\$135–235

Budget under NZ\$135

The prices are minimum
prices for a double room per
night without breakfast

PRICE CATEGORIES RESTAURANTS

Expensive over NZ\$40

Moderate NZ\$25–40

Budget under NZ\$25

The prices are for one meal

CONTENTS

DID YOU KNOW?
Timeline → p. 14
Local specialities → p. 28
Gone surfing → p. 39
For bookworms and film buffs → p. 45
Kiwi slang → p. 70
Lord of the Rings hype → p. 90
Blood-thirsty monsters → p. 107
Public holidays → p. 139
Budgeting → p. 145
Currency converter → p. 144
Weather → p. 146

MAPS IN THE GUIDEBOOK
(150 A1) Page numbers and coordinates refer to the road atlas
(0) Site/address located off the map
Coordinates are also given for places that are not marked on the road atlas

(⌕ A–B 2–3) refers to the removable pull-out map

INSIDE FRONT COVER:
The best Highlights

INSIDE BACK COVER:
Maps of Auckland, Christchurch, Dunedin and Wellington

The best MARCO POLO Insider Tips

Our top 15 Insider Tips

INSIDER TIP **Expedition to an animal kingdom**
Kayaking *at Nugget Point* with guide Jared Anderson to a seal colony below a lighthouse → p. 128

INSIDER TIP **Healthy eating**
The New Zealand TV show *Food Truck* is all about healthy fast food. New Zealand's mobile task force against unhealthy food is now based in Auckland → p. 36

INSIDER TIP **Hidden treasure**
A lake in a lake – where can you see this? On *Mou Waho* Island in Lake Wanaka a hiking trail leads to the light green *Paradise Lake* → p. 106

INSIDER TIP **Better than any leisure park**
Rere Rockslide is the name of a natural rockslide that ends in a rock pool. You can slide 70 m/229.7 ft downhill! → p. 50

INSIDER TIP **Fascinating underwater world**
Around the volcanic *Poor Knights Islands* the water is crystal clear and full of life. A diving paradise where you can even see whale sharks (photo top) → p. 40

INSIDER TIP **After the earthquake**
On the *Rebuild Walking Tour* through Christchurch with Kim McDonald you can find out about the progress with rebuilding the city → p. 76

INSIDER TIP **Just like in a film**
"The Light Between Oceans" was filmed at *Cape Campbell* lighthouse. You can sleep in the same cottage as Hollywood stars Michael Fassbender and Alicia Vikander → p. 99

INSIDER TIP **Wild beauty**
Karikari Peninsula is famous for its brilliant white and deserted sandy beaches. Kite surfers have ideal conditions here (photo right) → p. 44

BEST OF ...

FOR FREE

● *Free city tour*

In Auckland, volunteers enjoy showing visitors their city for free. A young actress who is vegan and a former TV journalist who is knowledgeable about urban multicultural society are among those working for *Auckland Free Walking Tours*. → p. 36

● *Creative microcosm*

The *Dog With Two Tails* is a café-bar with a small stage and old leather sofas in Dunedin where newbie bands regularly appear for free. Live jazz on Thursday is especially popular. Top entertainment for the price of a beer! → p. 84

● *Multifaceted Aotearoa*

Maori canoes, monster squid and Moa bones: *Te Papa Tongarewa* (photo) in Wellington shows what New Zealand is all about. The Kiwis' national museum has free admission and is popular for its fabulous interactive experience, e.g. a simulated earthquake → p. 64

● *Flipper for free*

Do you prefer not spending money on an expensive boat tour and want to see dolphins while swimming or surfing? Then head for *Porpoise Bay* in the Catlins. Here, there are plenty of curious Hector's dolphins that will jump through the surf with you → p. 84

● *Cinema – free and outdoors*

This is how you revive an industrial area: in the *Silo Park* of *Wynyard Quarter* in Auckland, where cement was once stored in 35 m/114.8 ft high silos, now films are projected free of charge onto the concrete walls → p. 36

● *Democracy live*

Women's suffrage since 1893 and a female Prime Minister who has a baby while in office: you can find out more about New Zealand's progressive democracy during a free guided tour through the *Parliament Buildings* in Wellington → p. 64

●●●● Dots in guidebook refer to "Best of..." tips

● Kiwis count

The flightless birds with long beaks and shaped like a hen are native to New Zealand. Sadly, predators imported from Europe like rats and cats have almost wiped them out. There is a good chance of seeing one of these birds at *Mason Bay* on *Stewart Island* → p. 108

● Kauri god

There are hardly any old buildings in New Zealand but instead the world's oldest kauri tree. *Tane Mahuta*, the 51 m/167.3 ft giant "God of the Forest" in *Waipoua Kauri Forest* is estimated to be 2,000 years old. Incredible! → p. 44

● Warrior dances

Before every game the New Zealand rugby team challenges the opposing team with a battle dance (photo). The *Haka* is an old Maori tradition and is a ceremonial dance performed countrywide in schools and sports clubs. Would you like to try? At the *Haka shows* in Rotorua spectators are allowed on the stage → p. 54

● A world before our time

What was it like in Wellington 500 years ago? It was quite like in *Zealandia*, one of the world's few ecosanctuaries in the heart of a city. While you stroll through forests full of rare parrots, you get a feeling of how things may have looked in New Zealand long before our time → p. 64

● Southern glow

Aurora Australis is the name for the spectacular light show in the southern hemisphere sky that you can see, if you're lucky, on *Stewart Island* → p. 108

● Bungy jumping horizontal

Plunging headfirst into the depths with a rope around your feet – that was yesterday: the *Nevis Catapult* in Queenstown is the world's biggest human catapult. If you get "strapped in" here, you will be propelled at a height of 150 m/492 ft up to 100 km/62 mi across a valley → p. 103

ONLY IN

BEST OF ...

RAIN

● *Excursion to the underworld*
In the *Waitomo Glowworm Caves* (photo) the green glinting glow of thousands of glow worms shines light in the darkness. Glide by boat through the grotto or go caving on a *Lost World Tour* deep underground → p. 59

● *Glimpse of the past*
How tough was life for New Zealand's first settlers? The *Toitu Otago Settlers Museum* in Dunedin offers some answers – here, the first gold diggers and sheep stockmen stare at you from among hundreds of old paintings → p. 82

● *A day at the south pole*
In the *International Antarctic Centre* on the outskirts of Christchurch you can withstand a snowstorm in a down jacket, watch penguins waddle through the snow or travel by boat to the south pole in the 3-D cinema → p. 77

● *Travel in the fantasy kingdom*
Enjoy a tour through the Oscar-winning *Weta Workshop Studios* in Wellington and see how "The Hobbit" or "The Lord of the Rings" achieved enhanced reality with special effects → p. 137

● *Historic cinema*
There are cinemas in New Zealand from the time when people said, "We're going to the pictures". Elegant Art Deco palaces from the 1930s with red cushioned seats and film-ready façades like the *Rialto* in Dunedin or the *Regent* in Hokitika → p. 84, 93

● *Pools with hot mountain water*
On rainy days, ideally you can enjoy Queenstown's majestic mountain world in the warm bubbling mountain water of the *Onsen Hot Pools* on the rocky cliffs above Shotover River → p. 103

RELAX AND CHILL OUT
Take it easy and spoil yourself

CHILL OUT

● *Excursions on the old tour route*

In New Zealand 100-year-old steamers are still in operation, e.g. the *Waimarie paddle steamer* from 1899 that still departs on river cruises along the Whanganui River. Or the *T. S. S. Earnslaw* from 1912 that departs daily from Queenstown for trips on Lake Wakatipu → **p. 68, 104**

● *Far away from world events*

The old Catholic mission *Jerusalem* is hidden away in the middle of lush vegetation in *Whanganui National Park*. Cows graze in front of the yellow-red wooden church and in the garden ferns overgrow the statues of Mary. Nothing is happening here. But that makes it so beautiful! → **p. 68**

● *Healing springs*

Relax and spend the day in the warm pools of the *Polynesian Spa* (photo) with a view of Lake Rotorua. No less than 24 pools are fed with healing water from two underground springs in Rotorua's thermal swimming pool. Although it's very touristy, it's still a wonderful experience → **p. 56**

● *Stargazing*

Gazing into the universe your own problems seem insignificant. Especially if you look into the night sky at *Lake Tekapo*. Hardly any other place in the world offers so many stars to gaze at → **p. 75**

● *Immersed in unspoilt nature*

Along the Marlborough Sounds many lodges are hidden amidst unspoilt nature that can only be reached by boat. E.g. *Nydia Bay Lodge* where you can stay overnight in yurts or wooden cottages → **p. 100**

● *City oasis*

In *Karaka Café* in Wellington there is a picnic atmosphere. On grassy terraces, the guests lounge on beanbags by the wonderful Whairepo Lagoon → **p. 65**

INTRODUCTION

DISCOVER
NEW ZEALAND!

Here, everything is still young and fresh. At the tip of the green *fern's frond*, the sunshine is reflected in the dew, while the waves break behind on the white sandy beach. Screeching seabirds hunt fish in the blue sea. *Rainforest* surrounds the long *glaciers*, deep fjords and lakes reflect snow-covered mountain peaks and volcanoes soar into the steel blue sky. Nature's forces break through the earth's surface; in some places the odours are powerful – like rotten eggs, and *sulphurous mists*. New Zealand is so *versatile* like a pocket-size version of Europe, a small country, which is still about 11,600 mi² bigger than the United Kingdom, although its population of approximately 4.8 million is not even a tenth of the UK population.

Admittedly, it's not exactly around the corner. When you're finally here, you will need time to relax and unwind. But anyone who has travelled on two *long-haul flights,* each about 11 hours, and has overcome jetlag will find a fabulous and versatile travel destination. It has an excellent tourist network of accommodation, easy transport and plenty of attractions for almost *4 million visitors* per year. The country at the bottom of the world is no longer an insider's tip –

Where politicians are busy bees: Wellington's "Beehive" with adjacent Parliament Buildings

sorry! But it's still breathtakingly beautiful here, even if the main attractions in New Zealand's high summer season from December to February are *jam-packed*.

No matter whether it's with hiking boots, in fins or snowboard boots – active holidaymakers can enjoy a great adventure here. You can hike across the entire country on the new *Te Araroa Walkway* or tour by bike on the Great Cycle Track – from Cape Reinga in the north as far as Bluff in the extreme south. The *national parks* include nine Great Walks and numerous shorter hiking trails and many other natural wonders. New Zealanders often enjoy exploring nature – *"going bush"* is not only a popular pastime for tourists. If you want more excitement, you can leap off bridges, out of a plane or from a cliff – and expect impressive views. The climate is *moderate and European*, and the Kiwis – as the locals call themselves – are very friendly.

approx. 925
According to Maori tradition, the legendary Polynesian mariner Kupe discovered the islands by canoe. The first Polynesians arrive on land in the 13th century. They travel in large canoes from the South Pacific and call the islands Aotearoa, land of the long white cloud

1642
The Dutchman Abel Tasman is the first European to discover the islands and annexes Nova Zeelandia for his homeland

1769
The English explorer James Cook arrives on land in Gisborne and lays

Everything is easy to discover here: the Pacific ocean in the east, the *Tasman Sea* in the west and in-between North and South Island, and hundreds of smaller islands dotted in the sea around them. In the partly *subtropical north* the holiday excursions are packed to the rainforests, beaches and lakes, volcanoes and green mountains. On South Island, things are more ethnic – here, you find Alpine mountains, glaciers and fjords and an unfathomably vast and versatile hiking and mountaineering paradise. The *Fiordland* is one of the country's three Unesco World Natural Heritage Sites. And then the *coasts* – together these cover more than 16,000 km/10,000 mi. In New Zealand, you will never be more than 120 km/75 mi away from the sea; if you hanker after salty air, you'll be happy almost everywhere in just a few hours – on a surf board, kayak or *stand-up paddle board* you can brave the waves. Incidentally, the 44 marine reserves are all "no take" zones, so you are not allowed to remove anything from here. You should leave the beautiful shells on the beach! You can also find city life here, although this is restricted to *Auckland*, which is the biggest city in the north on North Island, and the capital city *Wellington* on the southern tip. Christchurch and Dunedin in the south are fairly small.

> **Powerful forces of nature shaped the earth's landscape**

New Zealand's animals are legends. There are *cute birds*, which prefer to walk rather than fly, not only the kiwi, which shares the same name as the islands' residents. Rare dolphins play with surfers in the waves, around the islands there are plenty of *whales*, seals and numerous seabird species. Anything dangerous? No way! Unlike the oceanic Australian neighbour, in New Zealand you can expect plenty of unique species that are usually *absolutely harmless* and look genuinely cute. Okay, except perhaps for the scary weta, a fat *giant grasshopper*, which could drop on your shoulder in caves. But they're harmless.

If you are interested in ancient history, it's best to choose an alternative destination. New Zealand is a *geological newbie*, one of the newest countries on the planet. It only separated 80–100 million years ago from the super-continent Gondwana. Thanks to its youth the country has one of the world's *most active volcanic fields*. *It rattles and rumbles* in different corners, and mini earthquakes are the

claim to New Zealand for King George III

1840
On 6 February, the Treaty of Waitangi is signed between the Maoris and the English. The treaty is considered New Zealand's founding document. From now on the country is under British rule. The Maoris are granted the privileges of British citizens and some rights. At the same time, the New Zealand Company purchases Maori land that is sold to European settlers

1893
New Zealand is the first country worldwide to introduce women's suffrage

norm. The thermal regions around *Rotorua* on North Island will certainly take your breath away – and not only because of the powerful stench here. If you are interested, in this region you can gain a deep insight into the culture of the self-confident Maori, with *Haka, Hongi and Powhiri* – i.e. the warrior dance, touching noses and welcome ceremony. According to Maori tradition, Kupe, the legendary Polynesian mariner was said to have been the first to discover New Zealand and named the islands "Aotearoa" – *land of the long white cloud*, from now on the Maori name for their (new) home. The first immigrants

New Zealand is no budget travel destination

with their canoes arrived from the South Pacific in the 13th century; nowadays, the culture of the proud Maori, whose population is estimated as 735,000, enjoys a comparatively high status in the country. The *Treaty of Waitangi* in 1840 established sovereignty of the British Crown and the indigenous population. European settlers had discovered the green, fertile paradise in the 18th century and immediately recognized its economic benefit. The consequence: military conflicts and until today *disputed territorial claims*. In a country, which offers abundant space, land ownership is traditionally disputed. In Auckland *land and real estate prices* are the highest in the world. The cost of living is very high: New Zealand is not a budget travel destination. Many things have to be transported far across the world. The cost even of local products is often higher. Don't be surprised if *Sauvignon Blanc* from Marlborough is more expensive than back home. The Kiwis love drinking wine or beer. They don't have many other treats. With an average income of about NZ$49,000 (approx. US$33,000/£25,000) many people have high debts and often need a *second job* to make ends meet somehow.

Politically, New Zealand is still a member of the Commonwealth, the Queen is the *representative head of state*. However, the country is governed independently of the crown; so, many people demand full independence from Great Britain. During the 2017 parliamentary elections there was a *major political change* from the Conservative National Party to a coalition of Labour, the nationalist-populist NZ First and the Greens. Prime Minister Jacinda Ardern governs the country from the capital city Wellington. She earned immense international respect for her reaction to the right-wing extremist attacks on two mosques in Christchurch in March 2019.

1985
The New Zealand government declares Aotearoa as the world's first nuclear weapons-free zone

1986
New Zealand asserts political and legal independence from Great Britain, but remains in the Commonwealth with the Queen as its representative head of state

2019
On 15 March, an Australian right-wing extremist attacked two mosques in Christchurch; 51 people lost their lives

Despite the Kiwis' love of nature, the image of clean and green New Zealand unfortunately falls into the category of misleading advertising. The New Zealanders really *play catch-up* over environmental protection, especially waste management, banning plastic and protecting waterways. However, almost 90 per cent of the electricity supply is from renewable energy. Hydro- and wind power as well as geothermal heat are the main energy sources. The most important thing about your trip to the bottom of the world: take time to appreciate the country and people.

Probably New Zealand's biggest immigrant group: European settlers brought sheep with them

Slow travel away from the main tourist attractions shows you the real New Zealand. Along bumpy travel tracks and with the car covered in a thick layer of dust you find rustic locations, deserted beaches and down-to-earth,

> Kiwis love informal style, shorts and sandals are the norm

uncomplicated, informal locals who love to chat and sometimes invite tourists to the next BBQ. Please bring your own drinks! *BYO – bring your own –* is also popular in some restaurants. And you can stay *casual*! Nobody here needs to be too chic, not even in the evenings. The standard attire are shorts and sandals for every occasion and season.

New Zealand is a holiday destination for active nature lovers. But those who prefer to watch can also feel at home in the country – the main thing is being outdoors in the fresh air. There is *hardly any air pollution* here. That makes stargazing at the bottom of the world an unforgettable experience. So: take a deep breath! Then gaze into the sky and count the shooting stars!

WHAT'S HOT

Essential indie

Sound culture New Zealanders love their good independent bands that continue to tour the small clubs: for example, the folk singer *Aldous Harding* from Christchurch who was discovered busking on the street. The Kiwis also flock to concerts by the seven-piece band *Fat Freddy's Drop (photo right)* with Polynesian-New Zealand roots when they flood the countryside with Dub Reggae at one of the many festivals. "Young Blood" from the electro-indie band *The Naked and Famous* from Auckland is often played in New Zealand in bars and cafés. The singer *Kimbra* (with Gotye, she had the worldwide hit "Somebody That I Used To Know") and *Ladyhawke* ("Paris Is Burning") prove with their innovative electro tracks that tomorrow's sound is also created on the other side of the world.

1

Pimp your hut

Luxury in the middle of nowhere More and more New Zealanders are drawn to pimped-up wooden huts in the wilderness. For instance, *Bird's Eye View Cottage* – at an altitude of 1,000 m/3,281 ft in the Hunter Hills in South Canterbury, which you reach after a rollercoaster ride through the mountains. At the summit, the reward is an amazing panoramic view and heated outdoor tub. Or *Honeywell Hut* in Motueka, which looks like a gold-digger's hut from the outside – and inside is like an interior design magazine. In *Fossickers Hut* in the middle of the rainforest the Kiwis first go swimming in the wonderful Wakamarina River and then warm up by the cast-iron stove. *Woodpecker Hut (all four available on www.canopy camping.co.nz)* near Punakaiki is hidden in the rainforest and has an unspoilt view of the swirling sea – from the wooden hot tub on the terrace. The wilderness couldn't be more alluring!

2

Cowboys & steampunks

Fancy dress festivals   New Zealanders always find a reason to dress up. The country's biggest fancy dress party is the *Splore Festival* in Tapapakanga Regional Park near Auckland where every February the visitors celebrate DJs and bands in fabulous fantasy costumes. In Napier, at the *Art Deco Weekend (photo)* in February the whole town dresses up in 1920s style. In Oamaru, "the world capital of steampunks", men and women in Victorian costumes are not only part of the city scene in May at the *Steampunk Festival*. At the *Wild West Fest* in Waimamaku the cowboys are on the loose every year. In Russell for the *Birdman Festival* in July the locals rush into the water with paper wings and compete in the Dragqueen Race.

Spraying with life

Street art   The first graffiti after the earthquake in Christchurch in 2011 was a defiant attempt to bring some joy back to the collapsed city. Since then the best street artists in the world have transformed the centre into an open-air art gallery. This is why Christchurch is today also known as the *Street Art Capital (photo)*. *Watch this space (NZ$30 | watchthisspace.org.nz)* organizes tours to the gigantic wall murals. In Wellington, street artists working for the city authorities have given entire streets a facelift. The brochure *Secret Art Walk (Tourist Info)* highlights hidden art throughout the city. Even the small student town of Dunedin offers an amazing amount of street art. You can see the best artworks on the tour *Small City Big Walls (NZ$30 | FB: Dunedin StreetArtWalkingTour)*.

IN A NUTSHELL

ALL BLACK

Rugby is a religion, an institution and a cult – and the players are the *All Blacks*, New Zealand's national team and absolute stars at home. The small country towers above the rest of the world with three world championship titles. And that's all in black – the colour worn by Kiwi athletes at international events. The All Blacks have already buried many other teams' dreams of winning the title. These sportsmen are treated as legendary heroes and some of the All Blacks are top earners with over US$1.7 million/£1.3 million for a season especially in France. However, now the most popular active sport with young Kiwis is almost ubiquitous – football.

A QUESTION OF HONOUR

While rugby is a cult, down under sailing is simply a question of honour. New Zealanders are almost born with the tiller in their hands. And the Kiwis are successful at this sport too. It's not surprising – for a country surrounded by oceans that was first discovered by mariners. Auckland is not called "City of Sails" without reason. The Hauraki Gulf is on the doorstep – one of the world's best sailing grounds with optimal training conditions for pros as well as amateur sportsmen. In 2017, the New Zealand team won the *America's Cup* on Bermuda. The high-tech sailing regatta will therefore be another "home venue" for New Zealanders in 2021.

Photo: Letterboxes at East Cape

Where ferns offer silver shade and birds are flightless: what's special about the land of the long white cloud

NEW HOME

The modest country New Zealand is the dream home for more and more people. Almost 70,000 residents are accepted every year, mainly from Asia. The former classic immigrant destination of Europeans is undergoing major cultural change. As of the time of press, Aotearoa's population was about 4.8 million, Auckland is bursting at the seams. The biggest city with about a third of the total population accepts most of the new citizens. Most jobs are here, but there is not enough residential space. Many old Aucklanders are meanwhile leaving, so cities like Tauranga or Whangarei are booming. The government has now tightened the immigration rules.

NO SWIMMING!

Sad, but unfortunately true: more than half of New Zealand's lakes and rivers are not suitable for swimming. Water conservation in Aotearoa is inadequate in many places. The main problem is cow manure. For decades cattle could do what and go where they wanted – the dairy sector is New Zealand's biggest industry. The result is excessive nitrates in rivers and lakes. Therefore, more than half of all freshwater fish are threatened with extinction. Meanwhile, there are stricter rules for dairy plants, but they fall behind European standards. In addition, the countrywide deforestation of ancient forests in the past still has a negative effect today: during heavy rainfall many sediments are washed away from the unstable soil. On several beaches in Auckland the warning is often: no swimming! After torrential rainfall, the old wastewater plants regularly flood, and raw sewage flows into the sea. The stench is terrible!

IT'S BUBBLING UNDERGROUND

It rumbles, spits and bubbles in many places. New Zealand has one of the world's most active volcanic fields. Mount Tongariro spewed rubble and ashes in 2012 and its neighbour Mount Ruapehu erupted in 2007. In Auckland people are still asking when the next eruption will happen. Scientists expect another eruption here – but there is no reason to worry, as that can take another few hundred years.

New earthquakes are registered hourly on *geonet.org.nz*, as the country is not only on the Pacific Ring of Fire, but also on two overlapping tectonic plates – to put it mildly. The last major quake was at the end of 2016 in Kaikoura on South Island. Two people were killed, and the town was cut off for a long time from the outside world. Tourists had to be transported on ships and by helicopter – that's some holiday experience. In Christchurch, you can still see the aftermath of the disastrous and strong earthquake in 2011. The quake killed 185 people. The only positive side of these catastrophes: they highlight the Kiwis' solidarity; the tough New Zealanders' unshakeable optimism is impressive. If you live at the bottom of the world, you have to be resilient.

MY COUNTRY, YOUR COUNTRY

New Zealand's founding document is the Treaty of Waitangi. On 6 February 1840 the Governor of New Zealand, William Hobson, and about 50 Maori chiefs signed this document that regulated the country's government by the English crown. The Maoris were promised rights to their land, cultural treasures and protection from the British sovereign government. It sounded wonderful at first, but in reality there were heated conflicts and unlawful compulsory acquisitions from the native population. Another problem: there are various versions of the English translation of Te Reo from Maori. Back then, the Maoris knew nothing of the concept of "land ownership". The treaty's interpretation still leads to heated controversies today. Since 1975, the Waitangi Tribunal attempts to regulate controversial decisions. The Maoris have since then been paid large compensation sums and state territory has been transferred to their ownership again. For many *Pakeha* (those of European descent) the continuing compensation and special rights for Maoris go too far. This is a cultural and disputed taboo subject in the country. People always want to be politically correct. Kiwis don't like stepping on others' toes and avoid open conflict.

ONE OF US

The Kiwis are very proud of their Indie popstar Lorde. The singer song-

From soul to soul: the traditional Hongi greeting (without words) is a Maori sign of respect

writer is the top export hit from New Zealand. The Grammy award-winner comes from Devonport, a sleepy district of Auckland. Now, she jet-sets around the world and the hit lists. Croatia, her mother's homeland, is courting favour with Lorde and has granted her honorary citizenship even in her early twenties. The entire nation breathed a sigh of relief when the young New Zealand star purchased a house in Auckland. She chose her own artist's name; it was supposed to be simple but sound noble. But maybe Ella Marija Lani Yelich-O'Connor just had enough of having to write her name. That's understandable.

WHO OR WHAT IS THE KIWI?

Take care with the word "Kiwi". It means a New Zealander – it's a well-meant nickname. But it's borrowed from the name of a slightly plump, flightless bird with the long beak – the "kiwi bird". Then, there is also the "kiwi fruit" which originally wasn't quite so "kiwi". It comes from China and is the Chinese gooseberry. Most kiwi fruits are cultivated here, followed by Italy and then New Zealand.

SOUTH SEA TONES

Auckland is the secret capital city of Samoa. Most Samoans around the

Silver fern: New Zealand's tree-high emblem is still best seen in nature

world live here; there are almost three times as many as in their native capital Apia. Powerful youngsters from Samoa not only came to New Zealand because of their rugby talents, but also because of their energy. Until 1962, the South Sea state was governed by New Zealand and in the 1950s Aotearoa needed lots of workers. The Samoans mainly settled in the south of Auckland. Today, the rest of the South Sea community still meets in the district of Otara at the Saturday market: immigrants from Fiji, Tonga and the islands of Rarotonga and Nuie belonging to New Zealand. Those who want to visit the South Sea will do well to learn some *Talofa*, *Bula* and *Mālō e lelei*.

LUXURY HUTS

Living space was and is in short supply, particularly in Auckland. Kiwis are traditionally proud homeowners. Property prices in the city in recent years have risen to an average value of about NZ$1 million (approx. £500,000/ US$700,000) for a house. Often, the buildings aren't of exceptional quality. Properties were purchased by domestic and foreign investors like warm bread rolls and quickly offered on the resale market for high profits. Things have calmed down slightly. But the city still needs more homes because of the many immigrants, so building is going on at pace. Major traffic problems and a lack of infrastructure are at the back of the queue according to the motto: "She'll be fine!"

RARE ANIMAL SPECIES

If you want to relate impressive news back home, New Zealand's animal kingdom is a good place to start: rare animal species are not unusual here. Tuatara is at the top of the hit list – a 200 million-year-old tuatara species that only lives in the wild on some of the more remote islands. The small Maui dolphin can also be quite lonely with only about 60 of its own kind remaining, so he sometimes plays with the surfers in the waves of Muriwai. Incidentally, the rarest bird in New Zealand is not the kiwi but the flightless takahe with about 300 individuals – it is a wonderful blue bird that you can admire in several conservation areas. But the superstar among the flightless species is still the kiwi which is active at night. Its beak has touch sensors and its plumage is fluffy. Its shrill call makes it the animal emblem for the entire nation. Breeding programmes have boosted their numbers to about 68,000. Why can the kiwi not fly at all? Until settlers arrived there were no predators in New Zealand, so it would have been a waste of energy for the kiwis to fly. This made the flightless birds easy prey for new predators and over time they were almost wiped out. The DOC Nature Conservation Department is trying to systematically manage imported rodents, especially the possum: they are trapped, poisoned and run down. Even if they look cute, the New Zealanders' motto is: "Only a dead possum is a good possum."

SILVER FERN

It decorates the shirts of Kiwi sportsmen and women and is a wonderful route-marker in the forest: *Ponga, Silver Fern* – the big tree-fern is New Zealand's national plant. The underside of the frond shimmers silver so that it can mark the way at night. The Maoris once used the large fronds as roofs for their houses or to weave mats. The islands also have more than 200 unique ferns from tiny centimetre-long plants to the large tree-fern. The Maoris call the unrolled young fronds of a silver fern *Koru*. These spirals symbolise new beginnings and energy. You often find the Koru as a greenstone necklace, on tattoos and the logo of Air New Zealand. About 80 per cent of all ferns, trees and flowering plants in New Zealand are unique worldwide. "Let's go bush!", as the Kiwi says – the App *Flora Finder* will help you to identify them.

TOURIST BOOM

Tourists wherever you look! New Zealand is extremely popular. So, don't be disappointed if you meet more tourists than Kiwis in Queenstown. In the popular tourist spots in high season from January to March, nothing is possible without booking in advance. There are no beds, no rental cars and no tour guides! Day-long hikes to the national parks like the Great Walks must be booked months ahead. During the 2017/18 season, 4 million visitors came. Many places cannot cope with the crowds. That's another side of the boom: small communities can hardly cope with disposing the waste and the increased traffic. However, the government has no money to raise the tourism budget. Those who try and avoid the crowds and want to head into the bush as a *freedom camper* still have to keep to the rules: wild camping is only permitted in designated sites, and you should also have a chemical toilet and waste water on board! If you're caught camping without permission outdoors, you can expect to pay a penalty of at least NZ$200. That's not being shy! And justifiably so.

FOOD & DRINK

You can recognize New Zealanders abroad by the fact that they have a jar of *vegemite* on the shelf: it's a savoury spread with a unique flavour. If you want to experience New Zealand with all the senses, you should taste the brown spread – exactly like *pavlova* (meringue pie with kiwis and whipped cream) and of course grilled lamb chops.

New Zealanders start the day like the Brits with a *cup of tea* with milk or a flat white – a blend of espresso and frothy film – it was invented by a barista from Wellington. (The Australians are wrong when they say that they came up with the idea). Breakfast at cafés in New Zealand can range from porridge with fruit and nuts, *eggs benedict* with av-

ocado slices, pancakes with caramelized fruits or freshly baked scones with dates. *Clean eating cafés* are also popular – they only use organic products and prefer vegetarian or vegan ingredients (chia seed dessert etc.).

On your travels you will find a fish & chips shop and bakery in every small town, the steak & cheese pies and *sausage rolls* are sold as snacks between meals. Take note of the many vineyards, historic pubs and kiosks along your travel route. New Zealand's biggest wine-growing area is *Marlborough* on South Island with its ideal climate. There is hardly any rain, the nights are cool and intense sunshine during the day – this produces especially fruity grapes. Connoisseurs can instantly spot the

Where Chia dessert meets green lipped mussels and steak pie. For fans of novel and traditional food, rice lovers and meat-eaters

pure and fresh flavour of New Zealand wines when they have a glass of Sauvignon Blanc, e.g. *Cloudy Bay*. You will also find excellent wines in the many vineyards in Central Otago. *Pinot Noir* is world famous; the vines thrive in the region's rich mineral soil. You can taste plenty of award-winning varieties at *Gibbston Valley* – and admire the view of the mountains.

The area around Queenstown and Wanaka is also well worth visiting for the many fruit orchards where you can buy apricots and cherries. At the Bay of Plenty baskets of *avocados* are at the edge of the road for bargain prices.

Every region has its own *craft beer* (e.g. McLeod's from Waipu or Garage Project from Wellington) and celebrates local specialities – *oysters* from Bluff, langoustines from Kaikoura.

The glass cabinets are filled with cakes, pies and salads and are also typical for New Zealand cafés. You should definitely try *lollie cake*, ginger squares or Kumara salad!

LOCAL SPECIALITIES

Belgian biscuits – They were once known as "German biscuits" and re-named Belgian biscuit after the war. They taste of cinnamon and ginger and have a pink sugar icing glaze and are filled with strawberry jam

Cheese rolls – Rolls made of white toast cooked in a frying pan with plenty of butter and cheese. A popular snack on South Island

Feijoa – An oval fruit with a green skin that tastes similar to guava and is often used in New Zealand as an ingredient for lemonade (photo left)

Fish pie – A pie made from smoked fish, eggs and mashed potato with a crispy cheese crust. A popular dish in pubs

Friands – A light almond cake with ber-ries that are often served with natural yogurt (photo right)

Green lipped mussels – The biggest mus-sels in the world are up to 17 cm/6.7 ins long and only found in New Zealand. They are sold fresh in the supermarket

Hangi – A traditional Maori cooking method where e.g. sweet potatoes, pork and pumpkin are wrapped in flax leaves or put in wire baskets and cooked for several hours in an oven with hot stones

Hokey pokey ice – An ice cream variety invented in New Zealand with vanilla ice cream and caramelized honey-toffee pieces

Kumara – Sweet potatoes. Popular side order for fish and meat dishes. Kumara pommes are a typical snack

L&P (Lemon & Paeroa) – Sweet lemon lemonade from the area Paeroa

Manuka honey – Honey with an anti-bacterial effect from the nectar of Manuka plant from the mountain regions of New Zealand. It should help prevent common colds

Paua fritters – Mussel fritters with egg and onions. Many New Zealanders use the mother-of-pearl shimmering shells of the pauas as soap dishes

Pikelets – Light mini-pancakes made from icing sugar and egg that are usual-ly served with whipped cream and jam

Pikopiko – Fern shoots from the bush that taste a little like peas and aspar-agus. You can taste them e.g. on the Maori Food Trail

Seafood chowder – Thick seafood soup with milk and butter

Whitebait patties – Whitebait and egg prepared as mini-omelettes in the frying pan and with a crab-like flavour

You constantly hear the phrase, "Shall we have a *barbie*?" in New Zealand because almost everyone has a *gas barbeque* in the garden the size of a DJ's mixing desk. Steaks and seafood are grilled on it. If nobody invites you: in many parks and even in playgrounds there are gas barbeques for public use. Most cafés close about 5pm. Soon afterwards, from 6pm the restaurants fill up for *dinner* (and they often close again around 10pm). In so-called *BYO restaurants*, you can bring your own beer and wine. What about a bottle of "Middle Earth" or *"Cat's Pee on a Gooseberry Bush"* with your meal? Both excellent Sauvignons Blancs are produced by New Zealand vintners who not only understand their craft but also know how to have fun. You can also enjoy a good meal in *pubs*. On the menu are usually hearty Old World dishes like shepherd's pie or roast lamb but also typical Kiwi dishes like seafood chowder and *steamed green lipped mussels*. However, the culinary habits of the first European settlers are not the only flavours that characterize New Zealand cuisine today but gourmet influences from around the world.

Sushi (mostly an XXL portion) is available on every corner and in most fish & chips stores (you should definitely try deep-fried scallops!) you will find Chinese food on the menu and in Auckland *excellent Indian* and Asian restaurants. You can find out about *Maori* food on foraging tours outdoors. For example, on the *Kai Waho Experience (www.kaiwaho.co.nz)* with Maori chef Tom Loughlin at Lake Taupo or on the *Maori Food Trail (maorifood.com)* through the bush near Rotorua with chef Charles Royal. Compared with other indigenous people, like the North American Indians, the Maoris had a much more difficult time

No snobs: in New Zealand you can enjoy first-class wines

finding food. They couldn't hunt buffalo, but had to make do with plants, birds and fish. Their whole existence depended on *being able to read nature*. Nowadays, only a few descendants of the first Maoris know how to do this, and they like to show how you catch eels and prepare *pikopiko*, the rolled-up shoots of the Moku fern – of course, over an open fire and under the stars.

SHOPPING

100 % KIWI FASHION

Have you forgotten to pack your sunglasses? Then, you can purchase a pair from New Zealand designer *Karen Walker* who creates trendy frames in all kinds of imaginable colours and shapes. New Zealand singer Lorde, Lady Gaga and Debbie Harry are fans of the brand. There are shops in Auckland, Wellington and Christchurch. *Adrienne Whitewood* is a new and talented designer who is inspired by Maori art and culture. She sells her clothes and baskets with traditional patterns in her boutique in Rotorua. The young fashion and jewellery label *Company of Strangers* from Dunedin is inspired by punk- and rock music and its collection is produced 100 per cent in New Zealand.

COOL ON THE BEACH

The sun intensity is extreme in New Zealand. Here, nobody spends the entire day on the beach in a bikini or swimming shorts, but also wears a dress or T-shirt e.g. from surfer labels like *Huffer* from Auckland or *RPM* and *Lower* from Mount Maunganui. *Piha Swimwear,* named after the famous surfer beach near Auckland, even sells bathing suits with long sleeves, which give extra protection against sunburn. All these brands either have their own shops or they are available in surf shops.

FASHION FOR OUTDOORS

Fans of the great outdoors in New Zealand have a wide choice of good and reasonably priced outdoor shops. In *Kathmandu* outlets there are light down jackets and fleece pullovers in a variety of designs. Prices are generally reduced shortly after Christmas. You feel perfectly equipped for trips into the wilderness in the soft-shell jackets and hiking boots from *Mac Pac*. Slightly more expensive, and more high value, are the merino jumpers from ✿ *Glowing Sky* on Stewart Island made from wool from the Southern Alps and produced locally and fair trade. The outdoor label *Icebreaker* also depends on merino wool instead of synthetic materials.

GREENSTONE

You can recognize New Zealanders worldwide from their jade necklaces.

Avoid the tourist knick-knacks – these souvenirs from the other side of the world are worth it

You are not allowed to buy the *Pounamu* (greenstone in Maori) yourself, but you should be given one as a gift. At least, that's the tradition. This is why jade is the perfect souvenir for friends and family.

Typical Maori symbols are the fish hook *(Hei Matau)* or the spiral *(Koru)* which is reminiscent of an unfurling fern. You find Pounamu especially in rivers around Hokitika on the west coast of South Island. The best greenstone artists also live here. In the carving studio *Bonz 'n Stonz* you can even get creative yourself and polish greenstones based on your own design. *Mountain Jade* also sells genuine Maori amulets in Rotorua, Hokitika and am Auckland Airport.

NATURAL & ORGANIC COSMETICS

Clear air, unspoilt nature and plants with unique healing powers: New Zea-land is the perfect place for finding natural cosmetics. Honey from the Manuka plant is full of proteins, vitamins and minerals, and it is therefore used in face creams. Being considered as a superfood for the skin the black fern *(Mamaku)* retains lots of moisture. Lotions with *bee venom* are said to stimulate the skin's collagen production and help to prevent wrinkles. *Rotorua Mud,* from deep below New Zealand's earth, supplies minerals and makes the skin seem smoother. The Maoris believe the oil of the kawakana tree has healing properties to help heal minor wounds more quickly.

Certified ⊛ organic cosmetic brands from New Zealand are *Wild Ferns, Living Nature, Moana, Trilogy* and *Oxygen Skincare.* They are available in most pharmacies but also in souvenir shops, at the airport and in department stores, e.g. at Smith and Caughey's in Auckland or Ballantynes in Christchurch.

NORTH ISLAND

Half and half or preferably one third and two thirds? You can decide for yourself how much of your holiday time in New Zealand you devote to both main islands – depending on your individual choices and preferences. The minimum time for the whole country is three weeks, otherwise it will get stressful. And don't just concentrate on the south. New Zealand's North Island, where most visitors arrive, is not only the country's economic centre but it's also a beautiful region full of contrasts.

Explore the white, tranquil sandy beaches in the east and black, wild coasts in the west of North Island. Discover genuine Maori culture and the hustle and bustle of city life in the me-tropolises Auckland and Wellington. Active holidaymakers will love the steamy, volcanic heart of the north that is surrounded by beautiful lakes, rivers and forests. There's definetely no time to get bored on North Island.

Of course, the south has very impressive scenery. However, it can be quite lonely there because more than two thirds of New Zealand's 4.8 million population lives on North Island and most of them in the biggest city of Auckland. So you should leave plenty of time for the people and enchanting beauty of North Island. And don't be led astray by the Maori legend that New Zealand's north is nothing more than a giant fish on the hook suspended from South Island.

Gentle in the east, wild in the west, lively in the cities. And in the middle it's steamy. The giant fish on the hook has so much to offer

AUCKLAND

⬚⬚ **MAP INSIDE BACK COVER**
(152 B1–2) (*MO H–J5*) **The location on the wonderful Hauraki Gulf characterizes Auckland and its people. Here, they are relaxed, positive and gregarious. Kiwis rarely allow things to bother them – and certainly not the constantly changing weather.**

Auckland is situated on the narrowest land strip between the Pacific and

🏙 **WHERE TO START?**
Sky Tower: Enjoy the best overview at a height of 382 m/1,253 ft! From the tower, you can explore the city centre on foot or enjoy more attractions on the *Auckland Hop On Hop Off Explorer Bus (NZ$45 | www. explorerbus.co.nz)* ab. The first hour is free at the Jellicoe Street Carpark (Beaumont Street) and afterwards costs NZ$6/hr.

Tasman Sea in the west, which can influence the constantly changing weather conditions. A fresh breeze always blows in the "City of Sails", so every Friday afternoon in Waitemata Harbour the sailing boats compete in the so-called Rum Race – you not only need to brave the water, commercial Queen Street reveals Asian influences. Auckland's cultural influence is less imposing than its versatile natural heritage that puts most things in the shade here. Thanks to over 50 (extinct) volcanoes the city is undulating and has plenty of green spaces. 40 minutes from

Mountain with flat summit: the top of Mount Eden reveals its volcanic core

but also be ready for après sailing and a few drinks. Tourists who are keen sailors are welcome on board, if they wish, and should simply tour the boats in Westhaven from 2pm.

New Zealand's biggest city with a population of 1.6 million was founded in 1840. After Russell was the capital city for several years, Wellington became the seat of government in 1865. To this day, there is rivalry between the two cities, although the focus is mainly on sports results and the number of cafés.

Auckland has many culinary highlights mainly in the sophisticated wharf district and in Ponsonby. Every city quarter has its unique multicultural charm – its southern districts reflect Pacific flair while

the centre you can go surfing in the west on a wild, black sandy beach and enjoy a lazy afternoon on the other side on its white sandy beaches. In the west, the green hills in the Waitakere Ranges offer magnificent and beautiful hiking trails (however, may trails were closed as of the time of press due to a disease affecting the kauri trees).

SIGHTSEEING

AUCKLAND MUSEUM ☆

You can make your first contact in this museum with New Zealand's culture from the Pacific settlers to the modern period. The impressive Neo-classical building with panoramic views of the city is also the war memorial. It is on the site of an old crater – today, one of the largest city parks with beautiful old trees and plenty of green spaces. You can opt out of the Maori exhibition which is more authentic in Rotorua or the Bay of Islands. But you should definitely visit the *Wintergarden (daily from 9am | free admission | Wintergarden Road)* with the collection of native ferns. *Daily 10am–5pm | NZ$25 | Auckland Domain | www.aucklandmuseum.com*

MOUNT EDEN ☼

The sheep on the green slopes of this former volcano are cute and deceiving about how hot things get below: the *Auckland Volcanic Field* just below the surface is still active. The question is not whether but when the next volcano will erupt. Not to worry, this should take a few more years yet. From the edge of the crater of the city's highest volcano

(196 m/643 ft) there is a fantastic view. Maungawhau – the Maori name for Mount Eden – is a sacred place for the Maori people. Visitors should therefore behave respectfully and not venture into the crater. *In summer daily 7am–8.30pm, in winter daily 7am–7pm | 250 Mount Eden Road*

SKY TOWER ☼

"The Needle", as the the Sky Tower is also known, is Auckland's icon on the city's sky line. The lift (NZ$29) transports you in 40 seconds to the viewing platform 220 m/722 ft above street level. There is a casino, bars and the *Orbit* restaurant *(daily from 11.30am | minimum charge! | tel. 09 3636000 | Moderate–Expensive)* with 360-degree panoramic views and revolving hourly. The *SkyJump (from NZ$225)* from the tower is advisable before dining – that's definitely better for passers-by! You leap feet first on this beginner's bungy jump and are secured by a belt around your middle. Slightly less adventurous, but with the same dizzy views, is the *SkyWalk (from NZ$150)* around the top of the tower– please note, it's outside! *Daily from 8.30 am | Victoria Street | www.skycityauckland.co.nz*

WYNYARD QUARTER & VIADUCT HARBOUR

See and being seen – in the modern harbour districts *Wynyard Quarter (www.wynyard-quarter.co.nz)* and *Viaduct Harbour*, Auckland shows off new stylish and first-class architecture. Enjoy a stroll through the residential and leisure quarter by the waterfront, treat yourself to an excellent meal in the modern *Soul Bar (daily from 11am | tel. 09 3 56 72 49 | www.soulbar.co.nz | Moderate–Expensive)* with views of the enviable luxury yachts in Viaduct Harbour. A bascule bridge leads further into Wynyard Quarter, where you can enjoy more reasonably priced and artisan food. In summer, in the adjacent ● *Silo Park (www.silopark.co.nz)* there are open-air films free of charge.

LOW BUDGET

The clue is in the name: on the ● *Auckland Free Walking Tours (Thu–Sun 10am, in summer also 2pm | walks start from Queens Wharf – look for the blue umbrellas! | 89 Quay Street | www.afwt.co.nz)* committed locals show you their home city during a three-hour tour – free of charge. However, a small donation is gratefully accepted as a „thank you".

Finger food and street artists – the *Night Markets (Fri 5pm–11pm | 116 Cuba Street, Sun 5pm–11pm | Cuba Street/corner of Manners Street)* in Wellington are crowded and have a great atmosphere with live music and reasonably priced food stalls.

How about a hot bath with massage shower? Relax and unwind in the *Spa Pool (Spa Thermal Park Taupo | Spa Road)* in Taupo, where the hot Otumuheke Stream flowers into Waikato River.

FOOD & DRINK

CASSIA

Finest cuisine! Modern fusion cuisine with various Asian influences – one of the city's best restaurants, also a groovy cellar location near the Britomart (station). *Lunch Wed–Fri noon–3pm, dinner Wed–Sat from 5.30pm | 5 Fort Lane | tel. 09 3 79 97 02 | www.cassiarestaurant.co.nz | Moderate–Expensive*

INSIDER TIP FOOD TRUCK

Fast food is popular in New Zealand, but because the portly Kiwis are not so healthy, the food truck with a star chef and camera toured the country to change the nation's eating habits to fresh, healthy fast food, which is tasty and reasonably priced. The TV series (with the same name) was a hit; now there is a permanent modern-rustic restaurant at the *City Works Depot* not far from the Sky Tower. *Daily from 11am | 90 Wellesley Street West | tel. 09 9 73 23 05 | www.foodtruckgarage.co.nz | Budget*

MEKONG BABY

South-east Asian cuisine in a modern atmosphere in the chic Ponsonby district. The aroma is of fresh herbs, chilli and Kaffir lime, the dishes are innovative and delicious. You should leave room for a dessert and sip on a Thai cocktail aperitif in the cosy bar with open fire. *Tue–Sun from noon | 262 Ponsonby Road | tel. 09 3 60 11 13 | mekongbaby.com | Moderate*

SHOPPING

Around *Queen Street* you can shop to your heart's content: fashion, outdoor wear, electronics, souvenir shops and supermarkets. You will find designer tion of fashion and sports shops, usually not with current fashions but heavily discounted. Tourists benefit from a free shuttle to Onehunga located 30 minutes way, see the timetable on *www. dress-smart.co.nz. Daily 10am–5pm, Thu to 7pm | 151 Arthur Street*

OTARA FLEA MARKET
A busy flea market Polynesian style with live music and South Sea atmosphere. Tongans, Samoans, Fijians and Maoris

Queen Street shopping hub. Was the Queen ever on "her" street for shopping?

fashion and handicrafts on *Lorne Street*, in the *Britomart District* near the station and on *Ponsonby Road*. New Zealand's biggest shopping centre at *Sylvia Park* in Mount Wellington offers a compact shopping experience with more than 200 shops.

DRESS SMART
For bargain hunters – New Zealand's biggest outlet mall with a good selec-

are represented with their food, jewellery, clothing and vegetable stalls. A multicultural experience! *Sat 6am–noon | Newbury Street | Manukau*

THE POI ROOM
"Made in China" is a foreign word here – the Poi Room offers New Zealand arts and crafts, jewellery and souvenirs – produced by local artists. Authenticity comes at a price, but the tasteful

It also looks inviting from the sea: evening hot-spot Viaduct Harbour

the best surfing spots in the country. Beginners should learn the art of surfing the waves from the pros at the *Surf schools (pihasurfschool.com, muriwaisurfschool.co.nz)*, the boards and wetsuits are also for hire here. Top tip: here in the west, surfing at sunset is simply great!

WILDLIFE WATCH

Orcas in front of the ferry terminal and dolphins in speed tests with yachts – all kinds of marine animals, even humpback whales and Bryde's whales appear here in *Hauraki Gulf* which is rich in nutrients. The informative, roughly five-hour *Whale-watching Tour* with *Auckland Whale & Dolphin Safari (daily 1.30pm | NZ$180 | 175 Quay Street | Viaduct Harbour | tel. 0508 36 57 44 | whalewatchingauckland.com)* comes with a guarantee: if you don't glimpse any marine mammals, you can join a second tour. On the cliffs in Muriwai you can admire the impressive aerial acrobatics of the wonderful gannets. During nesting time from August to March a lot is happening. You reach *Muriwai Gannet Colony* via a dramatic cliff path at the end of the beach, simply follow the stench and the screeching.

HIKING

The green *Waitakere Ranges* west of the centre offer over 250 km/155 mi of hiking trails through the New Zealand bush, past dams and waterfalls. In 2018, most of these trails were unfortunately closed because of disease affecting the kauri trees. Updates are available via *short. travel/neu8*. Short hikes e.g. around the informative *Arataki Visitor Center (daily 9am–5pm | 300 Scenic Drive | Titirangi)* were still possible at the time of going to press.

products are exclusive and original. *Mon–Fri 10–5.30pm, Sat 10am–5pm, Sun 10am–4pm | 130 Ponsonby Road*

LEISURE & SPORTS

SURFING

The wild west coast beaches with black sand are not for cautious bathing beauties. *Piha* and *Muriwai* are considered

ENTERTAINMENT

Pubs and bars are practically located within walking distance of the harbour: around the Britomart (station), Viaduct Harbour, Wynyard Quarter and in trendy Ponsonby.

PONSONBY SOCIAL CLUB
If you still have energy to go dancing after the sightseeing tours, there are DJs and live music at the PSC. A good dance floor atmosphere with relaxed bar. *Daily from 5pm | 152 Ponsonby Road | www.ponsonbysocialclub.co.nz*

TALULAH
A funky Tiki bar with roof terrace above the Chamberlain Pub. Here, tropical cocktails are served in a kitschy and colourful Aloha atmosphere. *Tue–Sat from 4pm | 120 Quay Street | talulah.co.nz*

WHERE TO STAY

Airbnb is booming in Auckland, as medium-priced good accommodation is rare. Large backpacker hostels or expensive, ugly high-rise hotels are the norm, unless you treat yourself to luxury accommodation.

JUCYSNOOZE
Practical, modular and good! The new budget option in the centre offers simple, clean rooms in green and lilac. If that's your style ... Casual hostel comfort in a quiet location with daily 30 minutes free WiFi, parking spaces and rooms with en-suite bathrooms. *13 rooms | 62 Emily Place | tel. 0800 42 77 36 | www.jucysnooze.co.nz | Budget*

QUALITY HOTEL PARNELL
A pleasant exception, about 10 minutes on foot from the centre in the peaceful city district of Parnell. Typical hotel feeling, but very comfortable and clean. *105 rooms | 10–20 Gladstone Road | tel. 09 3 03 37 89 | www.theparnell.co.nz | Expensive*

INFORMATION

I-SITE
Princes Wharf | 137 Quay Street | Shop 2, Shed 19 | tel. 09 3 65 99 14 | Atrium, Skycity |

GONE SURFING

When there's good surf, the smaller shops or cafés near the coast have very flexible opening hours. You have to get your priorities right. Especially after a winter storm on the east coast, almost everyone with a surf board or paddle board plunges into the waves. Tsunami warnings are often not taken too seriously. Some people take a sickie. Surfing withdrawal is said to have a depressing effect. If the boss is also a surfer, it can get a little embarrassing. It's fortunate that everyone looks similar in a neoprene suit. Surfing is a tradition here with young and old alike and you can always find a wave somewhere on one of the two coasts. In the surfing meccas on North Island like *Raglan (raglansurfingschool.co.nz)* or *Muriwai (muriwaisurfschool.co.nz)* beginners can learn the art of riding the waves.

Victoria/corner of Federal Street | tel. 09 3 65 99 18 | www.aucklandnz.com

WHERE TO GO

INSIDER TIP ▶ GOAT ISLAND MARINE RESERVE (151 D4) (*Ø J4*)

Put on the fins and open your eyes under the diving mask – snorkel with ancient snappers (the bigger, the older – and the ones here are really big!) around Goat Island near Leigh. Almost one-and-a-half hours (90 km/55.9 mi) north of Auckland is New Zealand's oldest marine conservation area directly on a narrow beach. The island itself is a nature reserve, there is no entry.

Kayak and snorkel hire *(www.leighby thesea.co.nz)* is directly on the beach. The *Goat Island Discovery Centre (Dec– April daily 10am–4pm, May–Nov Sat/ Sun 10am–4pm | NZ$9 | 160 Goat Island Road | www.goatislandmarine.co.nz)* up the hill has an interesting interactive exhibition about the marine conservation area.

HAURAKI GULF ⭐
(151 D–E 4–5) (*Ø J4–5*)

A giant water playground right by the "City of Sails" that extends as far as Coromandel Peninsula! Several marine conservation areas and about 50 islands are dotted around the gulf. Close by is *Rangitoto*, the city's undisputed natural monument and newest of Auckland's volcanos. The last eruption was about 600 years ago. The *half-day trip (NZ$33 | www.fullers.co.nz)* to the island is a combination of pleasant boat trip followed by the ascent of the crater (260 m/853 ft, approx. 1 hr) through New Zealand's biggest Pohutukawa forest, past lava cave. The view from the summit over Auckland and the gulf makes a 360-degree panoramic picture worthwhile.

Waiheke Island is perfect for gourmets and slow travellers. The second biggest island in the gulf with an area of approx. 35 mi² has green hills, small bays, vineyards and amazing houses. A mixture of rich and alternative Aucklanders live on Waiheke. *Ecozipadventures.co.nz.* offers the three-hour *Island tour (NZ$119)* incl. superfast zipline and nature trail. Afterwards, simply stop off at one of the wonderful vineyards, the delicious *lunch platters* e.g. at *Cable Bay Vineyards (cablebay.nz)* complement the magnificent view. More information at *www. waiheke.co.nz*. The ferries to the islands in the gulf depart several times daily, details at *www.fullers.co.nz*. If you prefer a detour to the past, you should join the three-hour ferry excursion *(sealink. co.nz)* to *Great Barrier Island* (see p. 122). You will discover New Zealand as it was 40 years ago with lush vegetation, beaches and not many people. Paradise!

TUTUKAKA COAST (151 D3) (*Ø H3*)

If you like the coast, you will love this area about 200 km/124 mi north of Auckland. For divers and snorkelers, the marine conservation area on INSIDER TIP ▶ *Poor Knights Islands* is simply breathtaking. The water around the volcanic islands is super clear and in summer warms up to 23 degrees. In addition to 120 native fish species, dolphins and giant kelp gardens, if you're lucky you will also see several tropical relatives like manta rays or even whale sharks. Along the islands' rocky coastline you discover unique underwater plants, reefs and *Rikoriko Cave*: you can explore the world's biggest sea cave under water, with kayaks or paddle boards. *Excursion boats (daily 11am–4.15pm | NZ$199 | tel. 0800 28 88 82 | aperfectday. co.nz)* depart daily from Tutukaka Marina to the islands about 20 km/12.4 mi off the picturesque east coast that you should take plenty of time to explore. Along Tutukaka Coast you find secluded green bays like *Matapouri Bay* and the excellent surf beach *Sandy Bay*.

are Ninety Mile Beach, ancient kauri forests, the remote Karikari Peninsula and Cape Reinga, New Zealand's northern tip – the North country is surrounded by secluded and uncrowded beaches.

The Bay of Islands comprises 144 islands – simply start somewhere in the green-white-blue paradise

BAY OF ISLANDS

(150–151 C–D 2–3) (ⁿⁿ H2–3) **Beware – this is a kitschy and beautiful picture postcard idyll: a green island landscape with white beaches in the blue ocean. The 144 islands of Bay of Islands are a paradise for sailors, sea fishermen and wildlife fans. Here, you can swim with dolphins, drop anchor in secluded bays or hike on solitary coastal paths.**

Paihia (pop. 2,000) is the bay's tourist centre where most tours depart. History fans in *Waitangi* can discover everything about the country's recent history, as this region is considered the cradle of modern New Zealand. Day trip destinations

SIGHTSEEING

RUSSELL (150–151 C–D3) *(ⁿⁿ H3)*
The sleepy town (pop. 1,100) today has a tumultuous history. For a while, it was New Zealand's capital city and the raw customs of the whalers gave it a reputation as the "hell hole of the Pacific". At *Christ Church (Robertson Road/Church Street)* dating from 1835 you can still see the bullet holes of previous battles. From ⁣ *Flagstaff Hill* there is a fabulous view over the bay and at *Waterfront* you can enjoy a beer in a historic atmosphere: the ⁣ *Duke of Marlborough (daily 11.30am–9pm | 35 The Strand | tel. 09 4 03 78 29 | www.theduke.co.nz | Moderate–Expensive | also 25 rooms | Expensive)* was the country's first pub licensed to serve alcohol. Today, you can also

enjoy a delicious meal with a panoramic view towards Paihia, which is only a stone's throw away by ferry. More information: *russellnz.co.nz*

WAITANGI TREATY GROUNDS ★
(150 C3) *(ᗡ H3)*

Here, the nation's adventurous beginnings are revived again in a kind of open-air museum. Five minutes outside Paihia, at the picturesque original showground of New Zealand's founding as a state, you will discover everything about Waitangi Treaty. The route to *Treaty House* leads through mangrove forests past a 35 m/114.8 ft long Maori 150-man war canoe made from two carved kauri tree-trunks. Every year, on 6 February, the canoe is launched for the celebrations of *Waitangi Day*. On the vast lawn area in front of Treaty House, on 6 February 1840, 50 Maori chiefs assembled with representatives of the English crown under the Governor of New Zealand, William Hobson, and signed the Waitangi Treaty that marked the country's rule by the British. The various controversial versions are displayed in *Waitangi Museum* at the entrance to the Treaty Grounds. The impressive *Whare Runanga*, the Maoris' house of assembly, with its carvings of ancestors from around the country illusrates the regional unity of all the Maori tribes. There are Maori shows several times daily with Haka, other dances and singing. *Jan–Feb daily 9am–6pm, March–Dec daily 9am–5pm | NZ$50 including video, guided tour, show, museum | 1 Tau Henare Drive | www.waitangi.org.nz*

FOOD & DRINK

Outside the main cities there is plenty of gastronomic variety. *Paihia* on the *Williams* and *Marsden Road* has the biggest choice. Here, the *Waterfront Restaurant & Bar (daily from 5pm | 4 Marsden Road | tel. 09 4 02 67 01 | waterfront-restaurant-paihia.co.nz | Moderate)* serves fresh fish and seafood – this is a small restaurant with excellent service and blankets, in case it gets too chilly on the ☀ veranda with the sea view. This café is cute: 🌐 *Orange Frog (daily 8.30am–3.30pm | 11 Selwyn Road)* with great coffee and homemade organic dishes.

LEISURE & SPORTS

BOAT TOURS

Going out and about on the water is a must in the Bay of Islands. The *Discover the Bay Cruise (Oct–April 9am and 2pm, May–Sept 10am | from NZ$149 | Marsden/corner of Williams Road | tel. 0800 36 57 44 | www.exploregroup.co.nz)* from Russell Wharf in Paihia is a half-day trip with plenty of highlights, including the *Hole in the Rock* that you can tour by boat in fine weather and with a lunch or swimming stop on the breathtakingly beautiful *Urupukapuka Island*. Or do you prefer to swim with dolphins? *Carina Sailing (daily 9.30am and 3.45pm from Pahia | from NZ$145 | tel. 09 4 02 80 40 | www.sailingdolphins.co.nz)* offers a six-hour catamaran sailing tour with snorkelling and BBQ. If dolphins are spotted, you get out of the boat into the water. Or you can relax on deck and admire the marine animals' amazing feats.

WHERE TO STAY

Paihia (paihia.co.nz) has the most accommodation options. ☀ *Abri Apartments (3 rooms | 10–12 Bayview Road | tel. 09 4 02 80 03 | www.abriapartments.co.nz | Expensive)* specializes in small, but high quality accommodation with attractive sea views, tranquil, but easy to reach the harbour on foot.

The *Bay of Islands Holidaypark (678 Puketona Road | tel. 09 4 02 76 46 | www.bay ofislandsholidaypark.co.nz | Budget)* is a real insider's tip and is ten minutes from Paihia: a rustic camp site with idyllic, super peaceful camping pitches by the river, simple cabins and holiday apartments. You will meet more Kiwis here than tourists. If you prefer to stop overnight in *Russell*, you can either take the car ferry from Opua or the passenger ferry from Paihia. *Wainui Lodge (2 rooms | 92d Te Wahapu Road | tel. 09 4 03 82 78 | wainuilodge-russell-nz.com | Budget)* here is small, pleasant backpacker's accommodation with comfortable beds.

INFORMATION

BAY OF ISLANDS I-SITE
The Wharf | 101 Marsden Road | Paihia | tel. 09 4 02 73 45 | www.northlandnz.com

WHERE TO GO

INSIDER TIP ▶ **AHIPARA** (150 B3) (*ω G3*)
Surfers' paradise about 120 km/75 mi north-west of Paihia. *Ninety Mile Beach* begins below the town in *Shipwreck Bay*. The bay is like a surfers' car park on days when the surf is high. Hardcore surfers even drive further along the rocky coast where one big surfing spot follows another. It's not worth trying this, as rental cars are not insured here nor on the beach. At low tide, you can drive along the endless sandy beach with sand buggies. But you should always keep an eye on the tides! Ahipara has an excellent *camp site (168 Takahe Street | tel. 0800 88 89 88 | www.ahiparaholidaypark.co.nz | Budget)* with cabins, self-catering apartments and youth hostel.

CAPE REINGA & NINETY MILE BEACH
(150 B1–2) (*ω F–G2*)
On New Zealand's northernmost tip, at

Lots of green, plenty of Maori art, not much paper: An open-air museum emerged around the Waitangi Treaty

You cannot see the sky for the tall trees: in the Waipoua Kauri Forest

☆ *Cape Reinga*, according to Maori legend, the souls of the departed live on and continue their journey to the legendary Hawaiiki, the land of their ancestors. The cape is a mythical place where nature's forces are powerful. Here, the Pacific and Tasman Sea meet and the view from the *lighthouse* is awe-inspiring. It's best to book an eleven-hour tour from Paihia to so-called Northland, e.g. with *Great Sights (daily 7am | NZ$150 | tel. 0800 74 44 87 | www.greatsights. co.nz)*. The trip is long. Over the last 90 km/55.9 mi the endless, usually empty ☆ *Ninety Mile Beach* lines the route. The tour buses also travel along the beach – including a sandboarding stop.

In reality, the fantastic Ninety Mile Beach is only 88 km/55 mi long – not quite as long as the name suggests.

INSIDER TIP ▶ KARIKARI PENINSULA
(150 C2) (*ጠ G2*)
No man's land: long, white sandy beaches and behind that sand dunes and lagoons. A few small towns, a wine estate and olive groves: kite surfers love this flat peninsula about 110 km/68 mi north of Paihia; here, it's always windy on one of the coasts. *Rangiputa* is situated on a flat lagoon which is perfect for beginners and keen fishermen. The *Reef Lodge Motel (8 apartments | 44 Gillies Road | tel. 09 4 08 71 00 | www.ree flodgemotel.co.nz | Moderate–Expensive)* directly on the beach has simple, practical apartments. The wonderful, crescent-shaped *Maitai Beach* on the northern tip of the peninsula embraces the protected bay with the same name. Please note: you should bring all your supplies with you! On Karikari, there is only one small snack bar where the word "fatty" gains a whole new meaning!

WAIPOUA KAURI FOREST
(150 C3) (*ጠ G3*)
Beneath the oldest and biggest kauri tree ● *Tane Mahuta*, the "God of the Forest", (51 m/167.3 ft tall, 14 m/45.9 ft circumference, and an estimated 2,000 years old), you feel very insignificant. The west coast of Northland is still regarded as Kauri Coast, even if most of these ancient giants were deforested by European settlers in about 1860. Explore the forest, which is located about 70 km/43.5 mi south-west of Pahia, under your own steam or book a tour with a Maori guide with *Footprints Waipoua (daily | from NZ$25 | tel. 09 4 05 82 07 | footprintswaipoua.co.nz)*. There are also night tours; if you're lucky, you will see or

at least hear a kiwi bird. The *Kauri Museum (daily 9am–5pm | NZ$25 | 5 Church Road | www.kau.nz)* in Matakohe explains the history of the trees which are under nature conservation.

COROMANDEL PENINSULA

(152 C1–2) (*∅ J–K5*) **Sand between your toes and in every crevice (of your car) – a trip to the beach is a must when visiting this beautiful ⭐ peninsula.** Whitianga is an ideal starting point to explore the bays along the northern east coast. A little further south around Whangamata, the wonderful surf beaches are inviting and in the west the protected sea estuary of the Thames creates excellent conditions for seabirds to spend the winter. In the middle of all of this are relics of the gold-diggers in a ravine surrounded by a green mountain chain. The ☁ gravel roads in the northern part of Coromandel offer adventurers with their own car magical panoramic vistas of the coasts below.

BEACHES

HAHEI & CATHEDRAL COVE
(152 C1) (*∅ K5*)
From the long white, sandy beach in *Hahei* on the peninsula's east side, there is

FOR BOOKWORMS AND FILM BUFFS

Hunt for the Wilderpeople – After the death of his foster mother, twelve-year-old orphan kid Ricky runs away from the youth welfare office to the New Zealand bush. The chubby boy knows rap, but he has no idea of survival in the wilderness. Fortunately, his grumpy Uncle Hec (Sam Neill) supports him. Buddy Movie (2016) by New Zealand cult director Taika Waititi ("Boy", "Thor") with magical shots of the scenery and typical Kiwi humour

The Luminaries – The novel (2013) by Booker Prize winner Eleanor Catton is set during the gold rush in Hokitika in the wild west of South Island. Over 1,000 pages, the story is not only about the hunt for gold, but also about finding true love. Perfect reading for the long flight to New Zealand

Top of the Lake – The dramatic mountain landscapes around Queenstown play the main roll alongside Elisabeth Moss (Peggy from "Mad Men") in the 1st series of the mystery drama series (2013) of the New Zealand Oscar winner Jane Campion ("The Piano"). As a policewoman, Moss investigates for the first six episodes the case of a missing girl – in a lonely region between the mountains and forests with Campion's poetic fiming

The Penguin History of New Zealand – New Zealand is one of the last places on earth to be populated by humans. But there is plenty to relate about the country's young history. From the first Maoris to colonial rule by the British and up to the present-day – the book (2003) by the historian Michael King conveys a deep understanding of the nation

a wonderful two-hour coastal hike to the picturesque *Cathedral Cove* with its cathedral-like limestone formations in the sea. If you  kayak *(various tours from* NZ$5. If the sand bubbling from the thermal water gets too hot, simply cool off in the surf – a wellness spa New Zealand style. You should start your pool-digging

It's easy even when you're all fingers and thumbs: do-it-yourself pools on Hot Water Beach

Hahei Beach | tel. 0800 52 92 58 | kayak tours.co.nz) to the bay, you can avoid the crowded coastal path and have an impressive view of the rocky coast from below. Parking in Hahei in the peak season can be a nightmare. A shuttle departs from the car park at the entrance to the town to the start of the Cathedral Cove Walkways. More information at *hahei.co.nz*

HOT WATER BEACH (152 C1–2) (*M K5*)
What about your own hot pool with a sea view? And one that you've dug yourself – according to the motto, the deeper, the hotter. That's easy on Hot Water Beach. You can rent spades on site for about

at the earliest two hours before or at the latest two hours after low tide, otherwise you will be relaxing with a snorkel! It's also best to treat this as a social experience, since you are guaranteed plenty of pool neighbours. Next to the beach car park you find a cute *art and design gallery and workshop (www.moko.co.nz)* about 1 km/0.6 mi from the extensive *camp site (790 Hot Water Beach Road | tel. 0800 14 68 77 68 | www.hotwater beachtop10.co.nz)*.

NEW CHUMS BEACH (152 C1) (*M J5*)
Wow! A 30-minute route from Whangapoua to a golden beach surrounded by forest where the incredibly clear water

splashes of Wainuiototo Bay. New Chums is among New Zealand's top ten beaches. That's well deserved, even if it is a bit off the beaten track in the northern part of Coromandel Peninsula.

WAIHI BEACH (152 C2) (*W K5*)

15 minutes from Waihi, which is rather dreary, is the extremely long sandy beach. You have impressive views on the 45-minute ⚹ *hiking path* over Orokawa Bay, where a long dream bay awaits. Simply park at the northern end of the beach and trek uphill. More information at *www.waihibeachinfo.co.nz*

FOOD & DRINK

COROMANDEL MUSSEL KITCHEN (152 C1) (*W J5*)

Green lipped mussels straight from the Thames estuary. A hearty beer garden atmosphere with home-brewed beer from the MK-Brewery, e.g. *Gun Smoke Ale* or *Gold Digger Pils*. 10 minutes from Coromandel Town. *Only in summer daily 9am–3pm | 20 309 Road/corner of Manaia Road (SH25)* | Budget–Moderate

MANAIA (152 C2) (*W K5*)

The stonebaked pizza is exceptional. Fish, meat and vegetarian dishes complete the offers. Popular with locals and tourists. *Thu–Mon from 9am | 228 Main Road | Tairua | tel. 07 8 64 90 50 | www. manaia.co.nz* | Moderate

WHERE TO STAY

THE CHURCH (152 C1) (*W K5*)

Not only the faithful count their flock: this former Methodist church dating from 1916 is in an idyllic location in the bush, about 500 m/1,640 ft from the beach. Various room choices, optional breakfast, dinner in the small *Bistro* (Moderate).

12 rooms | 87 Hahei Beach Road | Hahei | tel. 07 8 66 35 33 | thechurchhahei.co.nz | Moderate

THE LITTLE SHED (152 C2) (*W K5*)

Cosy self-catering shed with rustic, blue outdoor tub for a romantic soak under a starry sky. Super clean and the owner, Donna, has plenty of good tips for excursions. Watching the sunrise on Mount Paku is a must! *1 shed | 11 Tirinui Crescent | Tairua | tel. 021 17716 85 | Facebook: TheLittleShedNZ* | Moderate

INFORMATION

WHITIANGA I-SITE

66 Albert Street | Whitianga (152 C1) (*W J5*) *tel. 07 8 66 55 55*
126 Seddon Street | Waihi (152 C2) (*W K5*) *tel. 07 8 63 67 15*
www.thecoromandel.com

WHERE TO GO ON THE COROMANDEL PENINSULA

COROMANDEL TOWN (152 C1) (*W J5*)

A magnet for hippies, esoteric fans and bizarre artists – the sleepy place on the peninsula's west coast has a few pretty little houses in colonial style, cafés and galleries. Barry Brickell's gallery, a potter who died in 2016, is legendary along with his ☯ *Driving Creek Railway (daily May–Sept 10.15am, 11.30am, 12.45pm, 2pm, 3.15pm, 4.30pm, Oct–April also 9am and 5.45pm | NZ$35 | book in advance! | 380 Driving Creek Road | tel. 07 8 66 87 03 | dcrail.nz)* – a rustic narrow-gauge railway through the rainy New Zealand forest, a personal project by the talented nature conservationist with a café and gallery. The one-hour journey passes sculptures and crosses viaducts. Part of the ticket price is dedicated to reforestation.

KARANGAHAKE GORGE
(152 C2) (*∅ J5*)

In the green mountain landscape around Karangahake Gorge, which connects Waihi and Paeroa in the south of Coromandel Peninsula, elves or hobbits would be at home – there are fairy-tale views to the fern-covered river valley of Ohinemuri River. From 1870 to 1950, there were four gold mines in this area. On the *Karangahake Tunnel Walk (start at Karangahake car park at SH2)* you can hike at your own pace along the old tracks used to transport gold through the lush vegetation and the 1 km/0.6 mi old railway tunnel. You can feel like "Lord of the Gold Rings"!

INSIDER TIP PINNACLES TRACK ⋌⋋
(152 C2) (*∅ J5*)

A challenging day's hike in the magnificent scenery of the trekking paradise of *Kauaeranga Valley*, east of the Thames – with many rewards! The panoramic vista from the 759 m/2,490 ft tall pinnacles is breathtaking – and not only because after the four-hour ascent through the dense Nikau palm forest you are out of breath after crossing streams and rope bridges. After about three hours, you can enjoy a short break at the well-equipped DOC hut. The last 40 minutes to the summit are adventurous – chains and ladders help you over the dramatic rock formations. The ascent is less challenging, but your knees will appreciate the support of walking sticks. You trek up and down this same route or you can stop overnight in the Department of Nature Conservation (DOC) hut *(Pinnacles Hut | 80 beds | NZ$15/night | book in advance online! | www.doc.govt.nz)* and travel back via the *Billygoat Tramline* on an old logger's path.

WHANGAMATA (152 C2) (*∅ K5*)

Here, on the east coast of Coromandel, half-way between Waihi and Hot Water Beach, everyone runs around in surf shorts and flip-flops – authentic Kiwi beach life with sand, waves and a pleasant café scene in the town. *Blackies Café (daily 8am–3pm | 18 Ocean Road | tel. 07 8 65 98 34 | Budget)* near the beach is popular with the locals, not least probably because of the super-friendly service. On a INSIDER TIP stand-up paddle tour to Donut Island, which is actually called *Whenuakura Island*, you soon have a Robinson Crusoe feeling. On this round island, there are no sweet pastries, but right in the centre a turquoise-coloured lagoon that you enter through a rocky portal. *Surfsup New Zealand (2 hr | NZ$80 | tel. 021 2 17 12 01 | www. surfsup.nz)* offers a guided tour on a paddle board, so the shipwreck feeling is only temporary.

WHITIANGA (152 C1) (*∅ J5*)

With a little luck, in this paradise for sea fishermen, you will see a giant blue marlin (about 3 m/9.8 ft!) with the long spear, when the fishing boats land with their catch at the marina. If you prefer to see fish on your plate, you're in the right place in Whitianga. *Squids Bar & Restaurant (daily 11.30am–2.30pm and 5.30–9pm | 1 Blacksmith Lane | tel. 07 8 67 17 10 | www.squids.co.nz | Budget– Moderate)* serves generous portions of fresh fish and langoustines in a hearty ambiance. If you also want to explore the beautiful beaches in the area and stay a while longer, it's best to rent one of the many apartments. *Blue Marlin (12 apartments | 4 Buffalo Beach Road | tel. 07 8 66 00 77 | bluemarlinapart ments.co.nz | Moderate)* offers a large selection of apartments, some with a harbour view.

Green renaissance: a ride through the dense, reforested woodland with Driving Creek Railway

GISBORNE

(153 F4) (*M7*) Rise and shine! In Gisborne, you can watch the legendary sunrise – this is the first city in the world to see daylight! The town has a proud history – in the 14th century, some of the first Maoris arrived on land here. Captain Cook also first came to New Zealand here in 1769.

"Gizzy", as the 36,000 inhabitants call their town, is located in lucrative Poverty Bay, where there is plenty of sunshine, the vines grow and taste good and fruit orchards produce delicious fruit.

Only the hapless Captain Cook called it "Poverty Bay" because when he set foot on land, there was a skirmish with the Maoris, so the crew had to leave again without any new supplies.

Gisborne is situated in the eastern part of North Island, at the foot of the spectacular East Cape, which is surrounded by Maori settlements, picturesque bays and empty surf beaches. North-west of the city inland between the Bay of Plenty and Hawke's Bay is the giant nature park Te Urewera with its lakes and unspoilt forests. On the way south, the wine region Hawke's Bay is linked to the wonderful Mahia Peninsula.

SIGHTSEEING

CAPTAIN COOK STATUE

The British mariner follows you here at every turn – the attractive 1 km/0.6 mi

600 m/1,969 ft pier in Tolaga Bay. How many fishermen can fit here?

was once a Maori Pa – a fortified village. You can either make the ascent along Queens Drive or enjoy a short workout and walk up the mountain *(1–2 hr return trip)*.

FOOD & DRINK

EASTEND CAFÉ
Small, inconspicuous café with surprisingly good dishes and excellent coffee. The most popular dish with regulars is eggs benedict! *Mon–Fri from 7am, Sat/Sun from 8am | 250 Marine Parade | tel. 06 8 38 60 70 | Budget*

THE WHARF BAR & GRILL
Cultivated atmosphere located in the Inner Harbour where the wine instantly tastes even better with a view of the great yachts. Versatile menu, breakfast also served on weekends. *Tue–Fri from 11am, Sat/Sun from 9am | 60 The Esplanade | tel. 06 2 81 00 35 | www.wharfbar. co.nz | Moderate*

BEACHES & LEISURE

INSIDERTIP RERE ROCKSLIDE
(153 E4) *(∅ L7)*
If you love waterslides, about 50 km/31.1 mi north-west of Gisborne you will find your paradise: you can slide for 70 m/229.7 ft on the natural rockslide in a natural rock pool. If you feel all the rocks on the slide, a boogie board or air mattress are recommended. The most applause goes to people who slide backwards. *Public access | Wharekopae Road | Ngatapa*

BEACHES
The city beach *Waikanae* is long and a very practical location at sunrise, but around the East Cape you will find much more attractive beaches. E.g. *Makorori*

long *River Walkway (starting at Waikanae Beach)* along the Turanganui and Taruheru River leads past the great explorer.

KAITHI HILL ☀
At the viewpoint on Gisborne's mountain, also called Titirangi Hill, you will find another Captain Cook statue, which is the joke of the entire town. Firstly, it bears little resemblance to Cook, and secondly his uniform is Italian. But the views are impressive and at the summit there are lovely, shady walking routes in the lush *Titirangi Domain*, where there

Beach; the legendary surf beach only 10 km/6.2 mi from Gisborne's city centre is also perfect for bathing beauties: a golden sandy beach with rock pools.

SURFING

You'll always find surf here somewhere. It's not surprising that some of New Zealand's best surfers come from Gisborne. The pros at *New Wave NZ* have surf boards for hire and give lessons *(Mon–Sat from 9 am | 189 Awapuni Road | tel. 06 8 67 14 39 | www.newwavenz.com)*.

TOLAGA BAY (153 F4) *(ŵ M7)*

The wharf extends for 600 m/1,969 ft into the sea in a beautiful setting with white cliffs, beach and river estuary – it's a popular photo motif and favourite spot for fishermen. The small coastal town about 55 km/34.2 mi north-east of Gisborne offers a *camp site (tel. 06 8 62 67 16 | www.tolagabayholidaypark. co.nz | Budget)* with huts directly on the beach and the historic, slightly old-fashioned *Tolaga Bay Inn (11 rooms | 12 Cook Street | tel. 06 8 62 68 56 | www.tolaga bayinn.co.nz | Budget)* is cheap and also attractive for backpackers.

WHERE TO STAY

PACIFIC HARBOUR MOTEL

A first-class motel for reasonable prices. A beautiful location on the Inner Harbour, it's only 500 m/1,640 ft over the River Walkway to watch the sunrise at Waikanae Beach. *28 rooms | 24 Reads Quay | tel. 06 8 67 88 47 | www.pacific harbour.co.nz | Moderate*

INFORMATION

GISBORNE I-SITE

209 Grey Street | tel. 06 8 68 61 39 | tai rawhitigisborne.co.nz

WHERE TO GO

EAST CAPE LIGHTHOUSE ★ ☆ (153 F3) *(ŵ M6)*

A lighthouse of superlatives – this is New Zealand's easternmost point. After that, it's out into the Pacific. The East Cape is one of the first places in the world to experience the sunrise. Early sport is also included – the ascent to the lighthouse includes 750 steps, which are exhausting, but the magnificent view along the green coast is really worthwhile. You cannot climb the 15 m/49.2 ft high tower.

You should allow plenty of time for the three-hour journey from Gisborne, which is 190 km/118 mi away; on your way is one fantastic beach after the next! It would be a pity not to explore them. If you want to stay overnight at *East Cape*, it's best to head for *Tokomaru Bay* or *Hick's Bay*. 40 minutes away from the lighthouse is the slightly outdated *Hicks Bay Motel (40 rooms | 5198 Te Araroa Road | tel. 06 8 64 48 80 | www.hicksbay motel.co.nz | Moderate)* with restaurant. *Stranded in Paradise (6 rooms | 21 Potae Street | tel. 06 8 64 58 70 | stranded-in-paradise.net | Budget)* is more inviting – a cosy backpacker's guesthouse in Tokomaru Bay, about 1.5 hr from the lighthouse.

INSIDER TIP MAHIA PENINSULA (153 E–F5) *(ŵ L–M8)*

Another genuine insider tip in Hawke's Bay is Mahia Peninsula's secret and about one hour and three-quarters south of Gisborne – it's off the beaten track and surrounded by dream beaches with crystal-clear water. You can explore the adventurous, gravel coastal route Kinikini Road past steep cliffs, green valleys and the view over the peninsula to the mainland. You have a fantastic panoramic view from ☆ *Mokotahi Hill* (20 minutes uphill) – the white rocky headland is a distinctive landmark of the peninsula. *Mahia Beach Motel & Holiday Park (43 Moana Drive | tel. 06 8 37 58 30 | mahiaholidaypark.nz |* Budget–Moderate*)* on the beach at Hawke's Bay has a small café. More information on *www. voyagemahia.com*

NAPIER (153 D6) (*₥ K–L8*)

Wine, cycle routes and architecture – at first sight the rather unremarkable Art Deco town of Napier (pop. 61,000) on Hawke's Bay has plenty to offer. It takes about three hours to get here from Gisborne. After the disastrous earthquake, which destroyed the bay in 1931 and killed 256 people, the city was rebuilt in three years with a typical "can-do" attitude. 147 Art Deco buildings were distributed across the city that now counts among the best preserved of its kind. You can download the *Art Deco Napier App (artdeconapier.com)* to cross off all the buildings. You can easily explore the city and beautiful wharf with a view of the distant Cape Kidnappers on foot or by bicycle (see p. 125). Information: *Napier i-Site (100 Marine Parade | tel. 0800 84 74 88 | www.napiernz.com | www.hawkesbaynz.com)*

In *Havelock North* (153 D6) (*₥ K8*), which is 20 km/12.4 mi away, is the first-class wine estate *Craggy Range Vineyard (253 Waimarama Road | www. craggyrange.com |* Expensive*)* with a newly refurbished restaurant – next to ☆ *Te Mata Peak*, which also offers a fabulous view of the surrounding valley and bay.

A further 20 km/12.4 mi south-eastwards and you can admire the aerial acrobatics of northern gannets at *Cape Kidnappers* (153 E6) (*₥ L8*). You can tackle the 10 km/6.2 mi long beach hike at low tide to the nesting sites of the *gannet colony*, or take a tractor ride with *Gannet Beach*

Adventures (from NZ$36 | gannets.com). The birds' nesting season is from November to February.

INSIDER TIP ▶ TE UREWERA
(153 D–E 4–5) (*₥ K–L7*)

A secluded, enchanting fairy-tale forest with a giant lake, waterfalls and impressive mountain ranges where you can easily get lost. It's advisable to keep to the well-established hiking paths. They start in *Aniwaniwa* – from Gisborne about 160 km/99 mi in a westerly direction, the journey will take you two-and-a-half hours by car. Since 2014, the largest native forestland throughout New Zealand is in the hands of the Tuhoi, a powerful Maori tribe from this region, whose members also call themselves "Children of the Mist". Early in the morning, when the mists rise over the

The beautiful Art Deco building has a sad history: an earthquake previously destroyed Napier

impressive *Lake Waikaremoana*, you also understand why. From Aniwaniwa you can go on day tours or a three- to four-day (hilly!) *Great Walk* around the lake with fantastic views. There are 40 Department of Nature Conservation (DOC) huts in the park that you can book in advance at *www.doc.govt.nz*, and the *Waikaremoana Holiday Park* (tel. 06 8 37 38 26 | *www.waikaremoana.info* | *Budget*) in Aniwaniwa also rents out huts. Incidentally, the name Te Urewera means "burning penis". According to Tuhoi legend, a sleeping chief got too close to the fire!

ROTORUA

(153 D3–4) (*Ø K6*) ⭐ **There is steam, hissing and bubbling and a smell of rotten eggs. Hold your nose and carry on because the geothermal phenomena in this region can leave behind a truly explosive impression because of the earth's thin crust that is under pressure here.**

Rotorua is located in the highly active *Taupo Volcanic Zone* and is also the country's Maori heartland. The ancestors of the Te Arawa People are said to have belonged to the first people in New Zealand and today their ancestors are very proud of their culture. Of course, the marketing emphasizes this – in Rotorua, the Maoris even take the lead and major tourism companies are owned by their tribes. Most of the region's thermal parks are also run by Te Arawa people. Typical cultural ideals are to put on a show and give an authentic description of their vibrant culture. The city on Lake Rotorua is surrounded by pine forests, dormant volcanoes and lakes. Obviously, the location (pop. 71,700) is a tourist magnet: "Rotovegas" offers the New Zealand full programme of nature, culture and adventure sports.

SIGHTSEEING

GOVERNMENT GARDENS & ROTORUA MUSEUM

Manicured gardens and English lawns honour the horticultural motherland in the *Government Gardens*. Free guided tours of the beautiful gardens take place daily at 11am and 2pm. They start at the central location of *Rotorua Museum*. The former city spa is today a showcase for the culture of the Te Arawa tribe and the history of the old bathing house. The attractive Elizabethan-style building with its half-timbered façade and distinctive red roofs feels like a building from a children's fairy tale on an XXL scale. *As of the time of press, the building was still closed due to earthquake repairs | Government Gardens | www.rotoruamuseum.co.nz*

LAKE ROTORUA

Lake Rotorua is North Island's second largest lake, and like most of the lakes in this region it was the caldera of a volcanic eruption about 140,000 years ago. *Mokoia* Island at the centre of the lake is a nature conservation area and a sacred place for the Maoris as well as being surrounded by a legendary love story. Because her father had forbidden Hinemoa to canoe to the island, where her beloved Tutanekai was waiting, she swam the 3 km/1.9 mi and followed the sound of the flute, which Tutanekai played. Today, the journey to the island is easy and fast with the *K-Jet Watertaxi (daily | NZ$99 incl. guided tour and visit to the hot pools | tel. 0800 5387746 | www.nzjetboat.co.nz)*.

SKYLINE ROTORUA

You can enjoy view from the gondola over the city and lake with a really generous New Zealand buffet. Calorie-counters can enjoy the return trip on the luge: the adrenalin boost on the concrete track burns up the calories. *Daily 9am–10pm | from NZ$31 | 178 Fairy Springs Road | tel. 07 3470027 | www.skyline.co.nz/rotorua | Dinner* Expensive

WHAKAREWAREWA & TE PUIA

The undisputed full programme in Rotorua: here, you can discover the extensive thermal region of *Whakarewarewa*, also called Whaka for short, as well as the spiritual and cultural centre of the Maoris, *Te Puia*. The *Marae* (assembly place), *Waka* (warriors') and *Pa* (permanent village) offer impressive examples of Maori architecture. The shows with traditional customs offer you some good infotainment: from *Powhiri*, the welcome ceremony, and *Poi*, the women's dance, to the ● *Haka*, the warrior dance that includes sticking out tongues to intimidate the opponents of the Maoris in true Maori style. Things are a lot calmer in the *New Zealand Maori Arts and Crafts Institute*. You can watch Maori artisans as they weave and carve. Whakas geothermal highlight is the 30 m/98 ft spraying geyser known as *Pohutu*, not surprisingly, meaning "explosion". In the 1970s the geyser's energy was siphoned off and the thermal energy used for traditional heating and cooking. This is now regulated, and the geothermal attractions are on offer. The Te Puia package includes boiling mud pools, hot stones and a *Kiwi Nighthouse*.

Guided tours (on the hour) are included in the price; the guides are members of the local Maori tribe. There are good combined packages – with guided tour, show and buffet with *Hangi*, the hearty and traditional Maori dish prepared and cooked in ovens under the ground: it contains Kumara (sweet potato), root vegetables and fish, chicken or lamb braised for 3–4 hr in natural heat. That's plenty of satisfying food!

FOOD & DRINK

CAPERS

Centrally located café serves an excellent breakfast and mouthwatering specialities like lamb in rosemary sauce and

Fairy-tale castle on a cauldron: Rotorua Museum is on very unstable ground

Daily 8am–6pm, in winter until 5pm | from NZ$54 for a day tour with various booking options, night tours also available | Hemo Road | tel. 0800 40 56 23 | tepuia.com

Tamaki Maori Village (daily 5pm, 6.15pm and 7.30pm | NZ$130 | tel. 0508 82 62 54 | www.tamakimaori village.co.nz) also offers a worthwhile three-hour cultural evening show with shuttle and Hangi buffet. As a glimmering bonus you can see glowworms on a short bush walk. Shuttle service from the hotel.

lemon tart as dessert. Not exactly cheap, but delicious. *Daily 7am–9pm | 1181 Eruera Street | tel. 07 3 48 88 18 | Moderate–Expensive*

TERRACE KITCHEN

Relaxed restaurant with unbeatable service and a central seaside location. Homemade light snacks, in the evenings heartier dishes like New Zealand lamb or the fresh catch of the day. *Daily from 7.30am | 1029 Tutanekai Street | tel. 07 4 60 12 29 | www.terrace.kitchen | Budget–Expensive*

SHOPPING

There are souvenirs here everywhere, like typical New Zealand charms, wonderful lucky charms with Maori symbols made from whale bones or jade. But make sure you check the origin of the jade: is it from China or New Zealand? The Maori experts at *Puawai Jade (daily 10am–10pm | 1174 Whakaue Street | www.puawaijade.nz)* carve gems from the local greenstone. With a tour behind the scenes at the workshop.

LEISURE & SPORTS

INSIDER TIP CANOPY TOURS

Swing through the tree-tops like Tarzan through the ancient, native New Zealand forest. This is a rarity in a country where the first settlers almost made sure of total deforestation. Part of your money for the three-hour tour over bridges and walkways with ziplines up in the tree canopy goes to support the operator's nature conservation programme. *Daily 8am–8pm, winter to 6pm | NZ$149 | 147 Fairy Springs Road | tel. 0800 22 66 79 | canopytours.co.nz*

INSIDER TIP KUIRAU PARK

Treat your tired holidaymaker's feet to a hot bath and chat with the locals in Rotorua's only public thermal park with mud pools, a small crater lake and hot springs. Always be sure to stay on the cold side of the fences! Rustic thermal relaxation in the city centre. *Free access | Lake Road/corner of Ranolf Street*

MOUNTAIN BIKES IN THE REDWOODS

130 km/81 mi of trails await you east of Rotorua in the magnificent Redwoods, a mountainous trail in the Whakarewarewa Forest around the beautiful blue and green lakes. There are different terrains, levels of difficulty and distances. Mountain bikes are available for hire in Rotorua from *Mountain Bike Rotorua (daily 9am–5pm | from NZ$35/2 hr | tel. 0800 68 27 68 | www.mtbrotorua.co.nz)*. More information: *Redwoods I-Site & Visitor Information Centre (Long Mile Road | redwoods.co.nz)*. Next to the Visitor Centre you can also go on a *Treewalk (daily 9am–10pm | NZ$25)* through the Redwoods – also with floodlighting in the evenings.

POLYNESIAN SPA ●

You deserve some relaxation! One of the oldest, but also most modern spa amenities in the town on Lake Rotorua benefits from various thermal springs. There are larger pools, private pools as well as family-size pools. You can also enjoy some treatments – e.g. mud massages. A private pool under a starlit sky in winter is especially romantic. *Daily 8am–11pm | private pool from NZ$20 | 1000 Hinemoa Street | tel. 07 348 13 28 | www.polynesianspa.co.nz*

WHERE TO STAY

In "Rotovegas" you will find everything from backpacker hostels to luxury lodges. And there is always a special offer somewhere.

COSY COTTAGE THERMAL HOLIDAY PARK

The genuine hot tip is rustic and traditional: camping spots with natural underfloor heating and simple accommodation by the lake – and no sulphurous smells! Water and heating use thermal energy; you can cook your own Hangi in a steaming hole in the ground or dig your own hot pool on the beach. The park's three hot pools round off the authentic experience. *10 rooms | 67 Whittaker*

Bilbo's dream location: in Hobbiton, the Shire lives on after filming is over

Road | tel. 0800 22 24 24 | cosycottage. co.nz | *Budget–Moderate*

IBIS HOTEL
An impersonal hotel complex, but with comfortable rooms and in a central location near the lake and city centre. Parking is no problem. You can happily opt out of the breakfast buffet, as it's better to enjoy a flat white just around the corner on Tutanekei Street. *145 rooms | Lake End | Rangiuru Street | tel. 07 3 46 39 99 | www.accorhotels.com | Budget–Moderate*

INFORMATION

ROTORUA I-SITE
1167 Fenton Street | tel. 07 3 48 51 79 | www.rotoruanz.com

WHERE TO GO

HOBBITON (152 C3) *(ff J6)*
If you like hairy feet and don't mind the 75 km/46.6 mi trip north-west, this pleasant spot in Matamata is ideal. You can walk through the original film set – the "swamp landscape" lives on here: the vivid round doors in front of the Hobbit caves with mini gardens in the middle of a sheep farm – the entire site nestles among green hills. Genuine Hobbit and Lord of the Rings fans naturally enjoy a beer in the *Green Dragon* by the crackling fireside. *Daily from 9am | NZ$84 | book in advance! | 501 Buckland Road | tel. 05084 46 22 48 66 | www.hobbitontours.com*

MOUNT TARAWERA ☇
(153 D4) *(ff K6–7)*
Have you always wanted to see an active volcano from inside? Then, join an adventurous day excursion to the crater. The one-hour journey east from Rotorua in the rustic 4-wheel drive bus is already thrilling, just like the ascent to the edge of the crater. Here, you are rewarded with a phenomenal view. Then, you slide on the solidified lava into the red crater.

It's better if you have sturdy hiking boots, as you don't need constantly to empty your socks! In 1886, Mount Tarawera first erupted for six hours; 151 people were killed, and the world-famous Pink & White Terraces were showered in ash.

itself doesn't have much to offer, the environment is beautiful. At the *Bay of Plenty*, where Tauranga is located, the sun shines more often and longer than in other parts of New Zealand. These are the perfect conditions to enjoy beach life

Unfortunately, no drinking: the champagne pool in Wai-o-tapu, the thermal wonderland

The last eruption was in 1981, so hopefully, only your feet should smoulder. Tours with *Kaitiaki Adventures (summer 8.15am and 1.15pm, winter 10.15am | NZ$164 | tel. 0800 33 87 36 | www.kaitiaki.co.nz)*

TAURANGA & MOUNT MAUNGANUI
(152–153 C–D3) (*K6*)

Tauranga (pop. 130,000), New Zealand's fifth largest city, 65 km/40.4 mi north of Rotorua, is hugely popular with Aucklanders who turn their backs on the expensive "big smoke". Now, you notice this by the traffic. The country's second largest port is here. Although the town

on the endless white sandy beaches, e.g. at the neighbouring *Mount Maunganui* with a view of the 230 m/755 ft high, extinct volcano *(on foot 1.5 hr to summit or 1 hr on the lower path)*. You can surf, play beach volleyball or sip coffee and enjoy the sea view, e.g. in ☆ *Deckchair Café (daily 6.30am–4pm | 2 Marine Parade | www.deckchaircafe.co.nz)*.
Or you can relax in the salt water pool: the recently refurbished *Mount Hot Pools (Mon–Sat 6am–10pm, Sun 8am–10pm | NZ$10.80 | 9 Adams Av. | tel. 07 5 77 85 51 | mounthotpools.co.nz)* offer various pools from 34 degrees. There

are shops and restaurants on Maunganui Road. The ⊙ *Mount Social Club* combines retro interiors with organic food *(daily from 8am | 305 Maunganui Road | tel. 07 5 74 77 73 | social-club.co.nz | Budget–Moderate)*. Make sure you leave room for the delicious dessert! The Mount, as the Kiwis say, is fully booked at Christmas, even the camping sites. The beach location is fabulous *Papamoa Beach Resort (535 Papamoa Beach Road | tel. 0800 46 12 22 | papamoabeach.co.nz | Budget–Moderate)*. Information: *Mount Maunganui Information Centre (1 Adams Av. | tel. 07 5 75 44 71 | www.bayofplen tynz.com)*

WAI-O-TAPU ⭐ (153 D4) (*∅ K7*)

Poisonous green, fire red and lead grey – the term "colourful" has a whole new dimension in this impressive thermal area covering 7 mi^2, and 30 km/18.6 mi south of Rotorua. The name means "holy water". You can explore the visually amazing spectacle of the *Thermal Wonderland* on three round tours (30, 40, 75 min). The *Lady Knox Geyser* is active daily shortly after 10.15am. Soap powder is added to the Lady, which offers extra entertainment during the short talk. *Daily 8.30am–5pm | NZ$32.50 | 201 Waiotapu Loop Road | www.waiotapu.co.nz*

WAITOMO GLOWWORM CAVES ● (152 B4) (*∅ J6*)

Excellent caving is on offer in the underground Waitomo Caves about 150 km/93 mi west of Rotorua – and twinkling glowworms take care of the illumination. New Zealand glowworms are not cute little creatures, but fairly unromantic, hungry larvae of the fungus gnat that can also turn to cannibalism. The hungrier they are, the more brightly they glow. Certain enzymes – known as luciferases

– make the larvae glow. You will find various tours through the three main caves by boat and on foot at *www.waitomo. com*. The absolute highlight for adrenalin junkies is the 4- or 7-hour *Lost World Tour (daily | from NZ$324 | tel. 0800 92 48 66 | www.waitomo.co.nz)*.

You abseil 100 m/328 ft into the mystical caves and hike through the labyrinthine cave system – past waterfalls and gigantic stalactites. If you prefer to avoid the crowds, you can visit the nearby smaller INSIDER TIP *Footwhistle Cave*, which is much quieter than the Waitomo Caves. *Cave World (from NZ$62 | 23 Waitomo Village Road | tel. 0800 22 83 96 | cave world.co.nz)* offers daily tours here for small groups, including a bush walk, and underground Black Water Rafting.

In the small town of *Waitomo* you will find fresh Asian and European cuisine at the *Huhu Café (daily from noon | 10 Waitomo Caves Road | tel. 07 8 78 66 74 | www. huhucafe.co.nz | Moderate)*, the ⤸ terrace offers a fabulous view of the green landscape with massive tree-ferns. If you want to stay, stop at the comfortable backpacker hostel *Kiwi Paka (11 rooms | Hotel Access Road | tel. 07 8 78 33 95 | waitomokiwipaka.co.nz | Budget)*. The location is very quiet, as Waitomo is secluded – apart from the tourism to the caves. Kiwi Paka has everything you need: fresh pizzas, dormitories or single rooms and rustic chalets.

WHITE ISLAND ⭐ (153 E2–3) (*∅ L6*)

The top attraction of the town of *Whakatane* one hour away from Rotorua in the east of the Bay of Plenty is White Island, a steaming, active volcanic island 50 km/31.1 mi from the coast that marks the end of the *Taupo Volcanic Zone*. Here, you imagine you are in Lucifer's living room – during the guided hiking tour of

Swashbuckler: you can get close to Huka Falls on the jet boats

the island you must wear oxygen masks and helmets, the colourful rock formations are like something from another world. And it stinks to high heaven! It's incredible to enjoy a 🔆 helicopter tour to the island with *Frontier Helicopters (from Whakatane Airport | duration 2 hr | approx. NZ$690 | tel. 0800 80 43 54 | www.frontierhelicopters.co.nz)*.

On the other hand, dolphins often accompany the boat tour to the island with *White Island Tours (duration 5 hr | from NZ$229 | tel. 0800 73 35 29 | www.white island.co.nz)*. Excellent combined packages with accommodation are available at the *White Island Rendezvous (38 rooms | 15 The Strand East | tel. 0800 24 22 99 | whiteislandrendezvous.co.nz | Budget–Moderate)* with a pleasant café. Whakatane is not an especially interest-

ing place, but in the east *Ohope* has an incredible, long surfing beach. More information at *www.whakatane.com*

TAUPO

(152 C4) *(𝄞 K7)* **Lake Taupo is deep, vast and surrounded by Maori legends. The lake defines the panoramic vistas and the open atmosphere of the town of (pop. 36,200) on its north-eastern shore.**

This region is truly sporting mad. It's not surprising – it's an outdoor paradise with opportunities for cycling and trout fishing, boat tours and excursions to the geothermal parks. The compact city centre also offers excellent shopping amenities. To get your bearings, it's best to park by the lakeside and admire the view over the snow-covered summit of Mount Tongariro. In the oldest New Zealand national park you can enjoy an adventure exploring the active volcanoes: hiking, mountain biking and even skiing.

SIGHTSEEING

CRATERS OF THE MOON
What's smouldering here? Make sure that it's not your feet and wear sturdy shoes for this thrilling excursion to the geothermal field about 5 km/3.1 mi north of Taupo. Two wooden walkways lead over 3 km/1.9 mi across the volcanic moon landscape with bubbling craters and steam fountains in the middle of the lava rubble. *Daily from 8.30am | NZ$8 | Karapiti Road | cratersofthemoon. co.nz*

HUKA FALLS
Huka means foam in Maori, and it's a fitting name. This thunderous waterfall

is five minutes by car from the centre – 220,000 l per second of the bluest water flows through a narrow ravine before it cascades in wild and foaming torrents about 10 m/32.8 ft deep into Waikato River. The ⚐ look-out from Loop Road offers a fabulous elevated perspective. Or you can get sprayed with foam in a jet boat *(NZ$115)* right beneath the falls. *Huka Falls Road | www.hukafalls.com*

LAKE TAUPO (152 C4–5) (*山 J–K7*)

It is fathomless and has a fiery history: at 186 m/610 ft at the deepest point and covering an area of about 240 mi^2 – slightly larger than the Isle of Man – Lake Taupo is New Zealand's largest lake. It was formed by a powerful volcanic eruption in about 180 BC. Explore the lake and the Maori rock carvings in *Mine Bay* 10 km/6.2 mi south-west of the city – ideally, during a sailing trip with *Sail Fearless (daily 9.30am, 12.30pm and 3.30pm, 2.5 hr | from NZ$29 | Taupo Marina | tel. 022 189 18 47 | sailfearless.co.nz)* or in a kayak (tour providers at the lake or on the local i-site).

FOOD & DRINK

DIXIE BROWNS ⚐

Here, you can dine from morning until evening with a lake view. The large selection ranges from wraps to pizza and hearty steaks if you are very hungry. The dessert counter has already tempted many visitors. *Daily 6am–10pm | 38 Roberts Street | tel. 07 3 78 84 44 | www.dixie browns.co.nz | Budget–Moderate*

REPLETE CAFÉ

The light and spacious café with a generous breakfast is a favourite rendezvous for locals and tourists. *Daily 8am–5pm | 45 Heuheu Street | replete.co.nz | Moderate*

LEISURE & SPORTS

CYCLING

From a level cycle ride by the lake to the single trails, or from a one-hour tour to three-day trail, with a guide or at your own pace – around *Lake Taupo* cyclists and mountain bikers are spoilt for choice. The top trails are the *Huka Falls Way, Great Lake Trails* or *Craters of the Moon Park.* More information is available at *www.greatlaketaupo.com.* Bike hire and pick-ups are organized by *Adventure Shuttles (504 Mapara Road | tel. 022 5 47 03 99 | www.adventureshuttles. co.nz)* five minutes away from Taupo.

WAKEBOARDING

You can try wakeboarding and water skiing for experienced skiers at *Taupo-wake Park (from NZ$35 | book in advance | 201 Karetoto Road | tel. 07 3 78 76 66 | www.taupowakepark.com).*

WHERE TO STAY

AMORI LODGE

This newer B&B in the city centre offers cheerful rooms with plenty of natural light. *4 rooms | 143 Heuheu Street | tel. 07 9 29 80 40 | amori.co.nz | Moderate*

SACRED WATERS ⚐

How about a lake view and your own thermal pool? These luxurious apartments on Taupo's waterfront are perfect. With a pool, fitness room, free bike hire and a garage. *15 apartments | 221–225 Lake Terrace | tel. 0800 72 27 33 | www.sacredwaters.co.nz | Expensive*

INFORMATION

TAUPO I-SITE

30 Tongariro Street | tel. 0800 52 53 82 | www.greatlaketaupo.com

WHERE TO GO

INSIDER TIP ORAKEI KORAKO
(153 D4) (*K7*)

The special thing about this thermal park in Hidden Valley 25 minutes from Taupo is the *Ruatapu Caves*, extremely unusual geothermal caves. The rest of the

Mount Ngauruhoe erupted 45 times in the 20th century; the last time was in 1975. The 1953 eruption of *Mount Ruapehu* killed 151 people. Other eruptions were less damaging, the most recent in 2007 caused a massive mud slide. The geothermal activity is constantly monitored, and the early-warn-

If you make the ascent by cable car, you can admire a fabulous view over Wellington

geothermal field with 23 active natural geysers, thermal springs, bubbling mud pools and vast limestone terraces is also fascinating. Included in the price is the boat tour via a small lake to the caves. *Daily 8am–4.30pm | NZ$39 | 494 Orakeikorako Road | www.orakeikorako.co.nz*

TONGARIRO NATIONAL PARK
(155 D–E 1–2) (*J8*)

The entrance is already dramatic: mystical and smouldering volcanoes with snow-topped peaks rise skywards from the vast steppe-land. Thick clouds scud past and their curious shapes constantly change. The region 100 km/62 mi south of Taupo is in perpetual motion.

ing system is effective. Nothing should happen, if you are skiing or hiking on the 2,000–3,000 m/6,562–9,843 ft high, active volcano. The ☀ ★ *Tongariro Alpine Crossing* is among the world's most popular day hikes. It takes between five and eight hours to cross the surreal volcanic landscape with incredible views. Please note: the summit can get crowded … The weather must be fine and the guesthouses in the national park organize the shuttle or from Taupo *Tongariro Expeditions (daily 6.20am | NZ$65 | tel. 0800 82 87 63 | www.tongariroexpeditions.com)*.

The INSIDER TIP *Taranaki Falls Walk* is a shorter alternative or suitable in bad weather: a simple, two-hour round tour of the volcanic landscape with views of Mount Ruapehu and a waterfall. The walk starts by the ⚡ *Skotel (48 rooms | at SH48 | tel. 0800 75 68 35 | www.skotel.co.nz | Budget–Moderate)*, a traditional lodge with backpacker- and hotel rooms, a sauna, shuttle, restaurant and view of Mount Ngauruhoe in Whakapapa Village. Hiking tours to the edge of the crater with *(tel. 0800 42 92 55 | www.tongariroguidedwalks. nz)* or without a guide are amazing!

The Maori chief Te Heuheu gave the park to the people of New Zealand in 1887, about a hundred years later Unesco designated Tongariro National Park both as a Unesco World Cultural Site as well as World Natural Heritage site. *Tongariro National Park Visitor Centre (daily 8am–5pm, in winter 8am–4.30pm | free admission | SH48 | www.doc.govt.nz)* in Whakapapa Village is a treasure trove of information about Maori myths, nature and volcanoes as well as the starting point for many hikes.

In winter, you can choose from two skiing areas: *Mount Ruapehu* in Whakapapa or slightly further south *Turoa*. The ski lifts also run in summer – for hiking enthusiasts who want to save time. Shopping and additional accommodation are available in the *National Park (crossroads SH4 and 47)*.

WELLINGTON

🔲 **MAP INSIDE BACK COVER**
🔳 **(155 D5)** *(𝄞 H10)* **"Windy" Wellington is one of the world's most stormy cities. The New Zealand capital (pop. 210,000) at the southern end of North Island is on the famous Cook Strait that is like a wind tunnel between North- and South Island.**

But you don't need to worry about constant bad weather here, because Wellington offers compact sightseeing with museums, parliament and parks and a feel-good factor. Plus, the restaurants are excellent – and all this is a beautiful seaside location. The *Sculpture Trail* on the waterfront also offers a walk past sculptures by New Zealand artists.

As a capital city, Wellington is fairly relaxed. City life is a successful mixture of the artistic and alternative set on *Cuba Street* and people in smart suits at *Lambton Quay*, the main shopping street, with the New Zealand parliament located at the end. Here, at least, you get the feeling of being in a metropolis. Perhaps, the relaxed atmosphere is explained by the city's location – on a geological powder keg. Wellington is close to the Wairarapa Fault and is one of New Zealand's most exposed cities to earthquakes – this is impressively recorded on *wellington quakelive.co.nz*.

CABLE CAR ⚡
The small, red cable car transports you from Lambton Quay 122 m/400 ft high to the district of Kelburn. If you want to enjoy the views over the city and harbour and find out more, you should visit the small *museum (daily 9.30am–5pm | free admission)* and learn about the history of the cable car or explore the galaxies above Wellington in *Space Place (Tue, Fri 4pm–11pm, Sat 10am–11pm, Sun 10am–5.30pm, in the holidays daily | NZ$12.50 | www.museumsswelling ton.org.nz/space-place)*. The descent back to the city passes through the attractive *Botanic Gardens* with dense vegetation and exotic plants. *Mon–Fri 7am–10pm, Sat 8.30am–10pm,*

WHERE TO START?
Waterfront: Leave your car on the waterfront and you're right in the middle. In the city everything is close by and many attractions like Te Papa National Museum and fabulous restaurants are at the harbour. From here, you can explore the city on foot or on the i-Site in climb aboard the *Hop-on-Hop-off-Bus (hoponhopoff.co.nz)* and tour the city for NZ$45.

Sun 8.30am–9pm, every 10 min | NZ$5/single trip | www.wellingtoncablecar.co.nz

MOUNT VICTORIA

From the local mountain at a height of 196 m/643 ft, you have a fabulous panoramic view over the region around Wellington, the harbour as far as Lower Hutt, Cook Straight and the (earthquake-proof) wooden houses on the slopes. Hiking and mountain bike trails wind their way up and down Mount Victoria to offer constantly changing and magnificent views. *Above Oriental Parade*

NEW ZEALAND PARLIAMENT

Beehive is the popular name for the 70 m/229.7 ft high, round concrete building where the ministries (naturally...) work diligently. The Beehive is connected to the *Parliament Buildings* and the *Parliamentary Library*. In the parliamentary chamber (like in Westminster) visitors can observe the public debates. 120 Members of Parliament make decisions here about Aotearoa's wellbeing, seven of them are representatives of the Maoris. The ● free guided tour of the parliament and library building is interesting *(daily 10am–*

4pm every half hour | reservation tel. 04 8 17 95 03 | www.parliament.nz) where you can admire the earthquake shock absorbers – when everything moves, at least parliament should be indestructible. *Molesworth Street*

TE PAPA TONGAREWA (MUSEUM OF NEW ZEALAND) ★ ●

The Te Reo Maori name for this ultra-modern museum, effectively New Zealand's National Museum, means "place of treasures". Here, there are manifold treasures: masks that illustrate the meaning of the *moko*, the Maoris' traditional face tattoos, dinosaur teeth and animal products, sculptures made from feathers, photos from the nation's founding era, works by contemporary artists etc. This is very entertaining and some of the exhibits are displayed interactively and they are free. The specialist areas at Te Papa are exhibitions about nature and Polynesian history, Maori culture and the country's geology. The exhibition about World War I, *Gallipoli*, is exceptional and was created by the director of "The Hobbit" Peter Jackson with the *Weta Workshop Studios* (see p. 137). There is an attractive shop and pleasant cafés. Plan at least two hours or more for your visit!
Daily 10am–6pm | free admission | 55 Cable Street | www.tepapa.govt.nz

ZEALANDIA ●

Kiwis, takahe and tuataras only five minutes from Wellington's centre: this nature reserve with traditional vegetation at the heart of the city is unique worldwide. On 30 km/18.6 mi of trails you can discover rare native birds, reptiles and insects like e.g. the *weta*, the scary giant insect that looks like a cricket, and rose to fame because of studios named after it. The 2.5 hr tour *Zealandia by Night (start at sunset)* is enthralling with an expert guide – if you're lucky, you will see or hear a kiwi; the bird is active at night. Includes a fascinating, multimedia guide.

like an old friend. Fantastic food with exceptional dishes like swordfish on risotto or grilled duck. The desserts are

That's not the head of the family, but the place that houses New Zealand's greatest treasures: Te Papa

Wrap up warm, even in summer! *Daily 9am–5pm/ NZ$19.50, Night Tour NZ$85 | Waiapu Road | www.visitzealandia.com*

FOOD & DRINK

Foodies who like to spend a lot or a little will be inspired here – Wellington boasts some of the country's finest restaurants and an amazing number of coffee roasting houses. On *Cuba Street* there are cheap eateries, whereas the nice restaurant on the *Waterfront* are pricier.

FLORIDITAS
A light, modern restaurant on Cuba Street, where every guest is greeted

good enough to lick off the plate! *Mon– Sat 7am–10pm, Sun only until 9.30pm | 161 Cuba Street | tel. 04 3 8122 12 | floriditas.co.nz | Moderate–Expensive*

KARAKA CAFÉ ●
Everything is Kiwi in this harbour restaurant: the music, decor and dishes – hearty Hangi, tender lamb and fresh mussels, which are served with wine or beer made in Aotearoa. You can enjoy the drinks outside in the sun on the comfy bean bags if you wish. *Daily breakfast & lunch, Fri/Sat also dinner | Taranaki Street | tel. 04 9 16 43 93 | karakacafe.co.nz | Budget– Moderate*

SHOPPING

You'll find fashion, high-tech and sports shops at *Lambton Key*, alternative art and knick-knacks on *Cuba Street* at *Iko Iko (118 Cuba Mall | ikoiko.co.nz)* or *Cosmic (97 Cuba Street | www.cosmicnz. co.nz)*. Authentic Maori artwork is available at the *Ora Gallery (23 Allen Street | www.ora.co.nz)* or *Maori Arts Gallery (1 Boatshed | Frank Kitts Park | maoriarts gallery.co.nz)*.

BEACHES

Wellington's best beaches are on *Island Bay*, *Oriental Parade* (close to the city) and ☆ *Lyall Bay* with views of South Island.

ENTERTAINMENT

Wellingtonians are good at partying. Most pubs and bars are at the *Harbour* or *Courtenay Place*.

LIBRARY BAR

If you run out of things to chat about, here are some alternatives. The quaint pub with tapas menu is packed full of old books. A quirky ambiance with interesting avant-garde cocktails. *Mon–Thu from 5pm, Fri–Sun from 4pm| 53 Courtenay Place | thelibrary.co.nz*

WHERE TO STAY

CQ HOTELS

Two hotels with different price and comfort classes under one roof right on lively Cuba Street – the Quality Hotel focuses on class, while the Comfort Hotel is simple and inviting. *115 rooms | 213–223 Cuba Street | tel. 0800 8 88 59 99 | www.cqwellington.com | Moderate–Expensive*

INSIDERTIP THE LIGHTHOUSE ☆

For romantics and everyone who always wanted to be a lighthouse keeper! This absolutely unique accommodation is in the quiet suburb Island Bay on the beach, 15 minutes from the city centre and offers clear, fabulous views of the coast. The small holiday apartment is rustic; breakfast included. The excellent *Beach House Café* is also just around the corner. *326 The Esplanade | tel. 04 4 72 41 77 | thelighthouse.net.nz | Moderate*

FERRIES

In stormy weather the ferry crossing to South Island is a bit choppy, in fine weather it's wonderfully relaxing. The ferry from *Interislander (from Aotea Quay, approx. 2 km/1.2 mi from the centre | tel. 0800 80 28 02 | 04 4 98 33 02 | www.greatjourneysofnz.co.nz/interislan der)* departs five times daily and takes about three hours to get to South Island. The competition *Bluebridge (tel. 0800 84 48 44 | 04 4 71 61 88 | www. bluebridge.co.nz)* departs four times a day from opposite the main station at Waterloo Quay. Pre-book car ferries in high season! It's worth comparing both ferry operators.

INFORMATION

WELLINGTON I-SITE
111 Wakefield Street | Tel. 04 8 02 48 60 | www.wellingtonnz.com

WHERE TO GO

KAPITI COAST (155 D4) (*∅ H–J10*)
Only an hour north of Wellington, you reach 40 km/24.9 mi wild beaches with small, charming towns surrounded by forests and mountains – the Kapiti

Coast. A ferry ride away is INSIDER TIP *Kapiti Island*, a nature reserve with numerous rare birds like the kiwi, kaka and the beautiful *saddleback*. The sea surrounding the island is also a reserve and if you're lucky you can see dolphins during the crossing. Two hiking trails lead to the 520 m/1,706 ft high ☆☆ *Tuteremoana*, the rocky coast is particularly spectacular on the western side. Visits to the island are restricted – you need permission from the Department of Nature Conservation DOC *(wellingtonvc@doc.govt. nz)* that you can apply for in advance by email. You should also organize in advance the boat trip with the *Kapiti Is-*

Otherwise, book the full programme from the second tour operator *(approx. NZ$185)* incl. Nature guide.

In *Queen Elizabeth Park* just behind Paekakariki on the Kapiti Coast, you can explore the endless sand dunes, surf, enjoy fabulous hiking tours or horse-riding with *Kapiti Stables (tel. 027 35 50 30 46 | www.kapitistables.com)*.

MARTINBOROUGH (155 D5) (*𝄞 J10*)

The pleasant town about 80 km/49.7 mi north-east of Wellington with charming old buildings surrounded by meadows and vineyards is in the wine-growing region of *Wairarapa* – in the

The rare kaka will appear – if you're lucky – on Kapiti Island

land Eco Experience (approx. NZ$80 | tel. 0800 43 37 79 | www.kapitiislandeco. co.nz) or *Kapiti Island Nature Tours (approx. NZ$82 | tel. 0800 52 74 84 | www. kapitiisland.com)* from Paraparaumu.

vicinity of some of New Zealand's most famous vineyards *Ata Rangi (www.ataran gi.co.nz)* or *Palliser (www.palliser.co.nz)*. Cycle tours to the vineyards *(greenjer sey.co.nz)* or a wine tour *(flatearth.co.nz)* from Wellington guarantee that you can also taste a fine drop. More information on the *Martinborough i-Site (tel. 06 306 5010 | wairarapanz.com)*. At ⚜ *Cape Palliser* an attractive lighthouse surveys the southernmost tip of North Island (1 hr from Martinborough) with lazy fur seals on the rocks. The arrival and view of the wild coastline offer countless photo opportunities.

WHANGANUI

(155 D2) *(𝄐 J9)* **Whanganui is a quiet town (pop. 40,000) with few attractions and mainly lives from the river along which it is situated – the Whanganui River. New Zealand's longest river (290 km/180 mi) crosses vast swathes of Whanganui National Park.**

You should take a look at the beautiful *St Paul's Memorial Church (20 Anaua Street)* filled with Maori art before you disappear in the lush vegetation of Whanganui National Park. You can either travel on the 1899 paddle steamer, the ● *Waimarie (daily 11am, every 2nd Fri also 5.30pm, approx. 2 hr | approx. NZ\$35 | waimarie. co.nz)* which departs from Taupo Quay in the city centre, by car along Whanganui River Road or gently by canoe or kayak.

SIGHTSEEING

WHANGANUI RIVER ROAD
(155 D2) *(𝄐 J8)*

Welcome to the middle of nowhere! Scarcely are you swallowed up by the rainforest of *Whanganui National Park* shortly after Raetihi at SH4 and you lose any connection to the present – you are likely only to meet the odd car travelling towards you on the winding road. Switch off the car engine now and then to listen to the loud crackling of the insects in the

bush. From Pipiriki (25 km/15.5 mi from Raetihi) the road winds 79 km/49.1 mi to Whanganui directly along the river, past Maori meeting houses with artfully carved façades and plenty of ⚜ viewpoints above the Whanganui River. Then, suddenly the old Catholic mission ● INSIDER TIP *Jerusalem (20 beds/ 1 double room | from NZ\$25 p. p. | tel. 06 342 8190 | compassion.org.nz)* appears in the middle of the luscious green. Cows graze in front of the yellow-red timber church and ferns overgrow the statues of Mary in the garden. It's easy to see how the nuns made their peace with the outside world in this fairy-tale location. You can also stay overnight: in a dormitory with bunk beds or a double room with bathroom.

"Jerusalem Daybook" is perfect nighttime reading; it was by New Zealand's most famous poet James K. Baxter who lived in the 1960s in a hippie commune on the Whanganui River. Fill the car with petrol before the tour and pack plenty of supplies!

FOOD & DRINK

THE YELLOW HOUSE

A yellow painted wooden villa with a beautiful garden filled with plants near the Whanganui River. Varied *All day breakfast menu* with quinoa porridge, eggs benedict or buttermilk pancakes. For lunch there are burgers, pasta and fish & chips. *Mon–Fri 8am–4pm, Sat/ Sun from 8.30am | 17 Pitt Street | tel. 06 345 00 83 | yellowhousecafe.co.nz | Budget*

LEISURE & SPORTS

WHANGANUI JOURNEY

That's the name of one of New Zealand's Great Walks that is actually a canoe tour.

Almost at home with the elves: a canoe tour on the enchanting Whanganui River

In 3–5 days, the tour includes the dense bush of *Taumarunui* (155 D1) *(⌀ J7) (about 160 km/99 mi north of Whanganui)* to Pipiriki, and is worthwhile completing in shorter sections. *Taumarunui Canoe Hire (from NZ$65 | 292 Hikumutu Road | tel. 07 8 95 74 83 | taumarunui canoehire.co.nz)* with its own freedom camp site, hires out canoes, reserves huts and camp sites along the route and collects you again en route.

WHERE TO STAY

INSIDER TIP ▶ FLYING FOX COTTAGES (155 D2) *(⌀ J8)*

Cottages built with great care from recycled wood that you can only reach by aerial cable car, the Flying Fox, across the Whanganui River. You must leave your car on the riverbank. On the other side of the river, you feel like you're in another world. For instance, when you chop wood to fuel the free-standing bathtub or dance to old Billie Holiday records in the evenings. A magical place. Overnight stays are also possible in glamping tents. *4 Cottages | 45 km/28 mi north of Whanganui | tel. 06 9 27 68 09 | www.thefly ingfox.co.nz | Moderate*

INFORMATION

WHANGANUI I-SITE
31 Taupo Quay | tel. 0800 92 64 26 | www.visitwhanganui.nz

WHERE TO GO

FORGOTTEN WORLD HIGHWAY (152 A–B5) *(⌀ H8–J7)*
Make sure that this road is not forgotten

by the world! The *State Highway 43* between Stratford and Taumarunui is far too beautiful for this. The highway continues for 150 km/93 mi through a fantasy landscape with green hills, ravines and waterfalls and past deserted coal mines as far as New Zealand's only republic *Whangamomona* that was already governed by a poodle. You don't believe it? Then, stop and ask one of the 170 residents. In the *Whangamomona Hotel (11 rooms | 6018 Ohura Road | tel. 06 7625 8 23 | www.whangamomonahotel. co.nz | Budget–Moderate)* the host even stamps your passport. Because there is very little traffic on the highway, you can drive more slowly in the especially beautiful spots – e.g. on the Tangarakau River, which flows through lush vegetation between high cliff faces. That's what the world must have looked like when dinosaurs still existed!

MOUNT TARANAKI/EGMONT NATIONAL PARK (152 A5) (*ω H8*)

At 2,518 m/8,261 ft, it is twice as high as Vesuvius and an extremely temperamental volcano: *Mount Taranaki* (also known as Mount Egmont) has not erupt-

ed for over 300 years, but near the summit the weather can change within minutes. However, tours of the lower slopes are easily managed. Above the *Dawson Falls Visitor Centre (Manaia Road | tel. 027 4 43 02 48 | www.doc.govt.nz)* in *Egmont National Park*, which surrounds the mountain, the 80-minute *Wilkies Pools Loop Track* starts. It continues through fairy-tale forests full of moss-covered trees to Kapuni River, where with a view of Mount Taranaki you can swim in the fossilized ☼ lava pools. The best place for photos of the volcano is the ☼ viewing platform at the *Egmont National Park Visitor Centre (2879 Egmont Road | www.doc.govt.nz)*. Between June and October you can also race down the volcano on skis and snowboards. About 1,500 m/4,921 ft below the edge of the carter is the small *skiing region Manganui (skitaranaki.co.nz)* with several drag lifts.

NEW PLYMOUTH (152 A5) (*ω H7*)

The city with a population of 56,000 on Tasman Sea is secluded but still in touch with the times: the *Govett Brewster Art Gallery (daily 10am–5pm | NZ$15 | 42 Queen Street | govettbrewster.com)*

KIWI SLANG

New Zealand dialect has some charming unique words that are not used in other English-speaking countries. Somehow, that's good. So, no worries. *Tramping* is hiking and you check out the area on a *tiki tour*. A *dairy* is snack bar, *bush* is a forest and *bach* or *crib* is a holiday home. *All good?* Kiwi English also has a special sing-song lilt. You'll get used to this after a while. *Yeah, right* … Then, there are

these charming colloquial expressions that reveal New Zealanders' general relaxed nature. *Chur Bro*, *sweet as*. (Meaning something like: that's alright, mate.) Te Reo (Maori dialect) is also an official language. In Rotorua, you're greeted everywhere with a cheerful *Kia ora*. *Kai* means food and *Koha* a donation. Te Reo is generally easy to pronounce with flat consonants and vowels.

New Plymouth has made a name for itself with culture: for instance, the modern Puke Ariki Museum

with its futuristic mirror façade is considered one of the top addresses for contemporary art in New Zealand. The interactive *Puke Ariki Museum (Mon–Fri 10am–6pm, Sat/Sun to 5pm | free admission| 1 Ariki Street | www.pukeariki. com)* provides an engaging insight into Maori culture and the history of the region. The city also stands out from the rest thanks to first-class restaurants, e.g. *Social Kitchen (40 Powderham Street | tel. 06 7572711 | www.social-kitchen. co.nz | Moderate)*, the 7 km/4.4 mi long *Coastal Walkway* at *Fitzroy Surf Beach* and one of New Zealand's best botanical gardens. The 129-acre *Pukekura Park (10 Fillis Street)* is an enchanting city oasis with tall trees, lakes, waterfalls and rowing boats. Bands regularly perform in the amphitheatre on the lake. More information: *New Plymouth i-Site (Puke Ariki | 65 Saint Aubyn Street | tel. 0800 63 97 59 | visitnewplymouth.nz, www. visit.taranaki.info)*

SURF HIGHWAY (SH 45)
(152 A5–6) (*ΩΩ G–H 7–8*)
On one side is Tasman Sea and on the other side is the volcanic Mount Taranaki with its snow-covered summit: along the Surf Highway 45 between New Plymouth and Hawera (105 km/65 mi), you will not be able to stop admiring nature. The following stops are worthwhile: *Oakura*, because of the many artists and surfers and the *Arts Trail (oakuraarts.co.nz)* with galleries and art workshops. *Kumera Patch*, where you get the best surf waves. *Komene Road*, because here beginners can also stay on the surf board.

SOUTH ISLAND

Fewer people live on South Island than North Island, but there are one million more sheep. There is also plenty of space because only a quarter of all New Zealanders (about 1.1 million) call *Te Wai Pounamu* **– the waters of the greenstone, as South Island is known in Maori – their home.**

The countryside is so empty that it's easy to shoot films here which are set in different centuries. Location scouts can choose between rainforests, snow-covered mountains, glaciers, isolated rivers, wild beaches, bright blue lakes and old gold-digger towns. In the morning, you can swim in the sea and climb a glacier in the afternoon. What about sleeping at night in the rainforest? That's no problem on South Island, where the landscapes are as different as the weather. It's not unusual to experience four seasons in a day. That also explains the typical look of South Islanders: a down jacket with shorts and plastic sandals.

Where does South Island win against North Island? There are fewer traffic jams (there are hardly any big cities) and definitely more lumberjack competitions (you have to while away the time somehow!). There are more national parks (nine out of a total of 14), the biggest ski areas, the best oysters, more hours of sunshine in the summer, but unfortunately also more Antarctic winds. In short: on South Island mother earth plays the main role and you're just an extra – against the backdrop of nature's magnificent spectacle!

Glaciers, fjords and lakes – spectacular!
The secluded nature of the South makes it a
dream location not only for fantasy film fans

AORAKI/
MOUNT COOK

(159 E1) (𝄞 D13) **Unfortunately, the
summit of Aoraki (Mount Cook), the
"mountain that pierces the clouds", is
usually hidden behind clouds.**
With a little luck, New Zealand's white
giant (3,724 m/12,218 ft) gleams in the
sunshine – and while you hike around
the country's highest mountain you'll
feel as if you're in heaven. From *Mount
Cook Village* at 750 m/2,461 ft, various hiking trails begin – and of course,
planes and helicopters, which fly you
to Tasman Glacier above the mountain
summit.

SIGHTSEEING

EDMUND HILLARY ALPINE CENTRE
From New Zealand's roof to the roof of
the world: the 3-D cinema with small museum at the Hermitage Hotel in Mount

HOOKER VALLEY TRACK

Wildflowers before the snow-covered mountains are not the only beautiful photo motif along the route. The 3-hour track through Hooker Valley in the direction of Mount Cook leads across several rope bridges, past the Mueller Glacier and ends at Hooker Lake where icebergs float. It starts off at White Horse Hill Campground at the end of Hooker Valley Road 2 km/1.2 mi from Mount Cook Village.

TASMAN GLACIER LAKE CRUISE ★

Lumps of ice constantly break off the Tasman Glacier and float like gigantic ice cubes around Glacier Lake Glacier. On boat tours you approach the ice giant and the gorge of the glacier and you can try the 300–500-year-old ice crystals (or whisky with glacier ice, if you smuggle a small bottle on board). If you want to save money: from the shore, the lake looks just as impressive. *2.5 hr incl. transfer from Mount Cook Village 10 km/6.2 mi away and 30-min hike| NZ$170 | tel. 0800 42 43 86 | www. relaxingjourneys.co.nz*

Lake Tekapo: in the day, its blue attracts glances, and at night, the stars above

Cook Village is dedicated to the expeditions of famous New Zealand mountaineer, Sir Edmund Hillary. A 75-minute documentary is devoted to his ascent of Mount-Everest and the film "Mount Cook Magic" about the mountain where Hillary learned mountaineering. *Oct–March daily 7.30am–8.30pm, April–Sept 8am–7pm | NZ$20 | Terrace Road*

LEISURE & SPORTS

The popular *Alps 2 Ocean Cycle Trail (www.alps2ocean.com)* starts at Mount Cook and continues for 6–8 days as far as Oamaru on the east coast.

WHERE TO STAY

THE HERMITAGE

It's classic: the hotel was built in 1884, but it was destroyed again several times. The newest building dates from 1957 and has been repeatedly extended over the years. Today, there are 〰 164 rooms in the luxury hotel with dream views of the snow-covered mountain peaks. At the entrance, a statue of Sir Edmund Hillary looks longingly towards Mount Cook. *89 Terrace Road | tel. 03 4 35 18 09 | www. hermitage.co.nz | Expensive*

MOUNT COOK LODGE & MOTELS

Bunk beds, double rooms with en-suite bathrooms, studios or chalets: the lodge offers rooms and chalets for every budget. The Chamois Bar with a large glass front, serves burgers with a mountain view. *50 rooms/164 beds | Mount Cook Village | tel. 03 4 35 16 53 | mtcooklodge.co.nz | Budget–Moderate*

INFORMATION

AORAKI MOUNT COOK NATIONAL PARK VISITOR CENTRE

Exhibitions with information about the area and tour bookings, helicopter flights etc. *1 Larch Grove | Mount Cook Village | tel. 03 4 35 11 86 | mackenzienz.com*

WHERE TO GO

INSIDER TIP LAKE OHAU

(159 E2) (*D14*)

The best thing about Lake Ohau, 85 km/52.8 mi south, is the tranquillity. There are no jet skiers, paragliders or parachutists far and wide. You share the pebble beach with a few sandflies, and the nearby mountains look even more majestic when you swim towards them in the light blue lake. On the lake shore there are several camping grounds for caravans with amazing views of the lake. The view from the rooms at *Lake Ohau Lodge (72 rooms | 2295 Lake Ohau Road | tel. 03 4 38 98 85 | ohau.co.nz | Moderate)* is just as impressive and there is a large panoramic terrace.

LAKE TEKAPO ★

(159 E1) (*D13–14*)

More touristy than Lake Ohau, but equally photogenic: Lake Tekapo gleams so light blue that you have to squint when you look at it. If the sun is setting, the ● sky shines particularly brightly because the lake, 125 km/78 mi south-east

MARCO POLO HIGHLIGHTS

★ Tasman Glacier Lake Cruise
Boat cruises among the icebergs → p. 74

★ Lake Tekapo
Light blue, sparkling dream lake – surrounded by mountains → p. 75

★ Kaikoura
Spot sperm whales and try freshly caught langoustines → p. 79

★ Catlins
Hardly any tourists, but magnificent nature with seals and penguins → p. 84

★ Glacier in the rainforest
At Franz Josef Glacier and Fox Glacier the ice meets lush vegetation → p. 87, 89

★ Abel Tasman National Park
Beautiful hikes through ancient forest and across beaches → p. 96

★ Marlborough Sounds
Fjord landscape with jade-green water and lodgings in the rainforest → p. 100

★ Queenstown
Thrilling and fun sports location on crystal blue Lake Wakatipu → p. 100

★ Stewart Island
Watch kiwis and collect photos of the flaming sunsets → p. 107

★ Milford Sound
Fjord with rugged cliffs and waterfalls. So photogenic! → p. 113

of Mount Cook, is one of those places in the world where you can see the most stars. On *Mount John* above the lake is the *Observatory (times and prices depending on season, e.g. Mt. John Observatory Tour, 2 hr, approx. NZ$150 | signpost at SH 8 | www.earthandsky.co.nz)* with New Zealand's biggest telescope. Nearby begins the wonderful ⚜ *Summit Circuit Track (30–45 min)* with panoramic vistas of the lake and region's mountains. You can sleep right by the lake at the *Lake Tekapo Motels & Holiday Park (2 Lakeside Drive | tel. 0800 85 38 53 | laketekapo-accommodation.co.nz | Budget)*, either in your own tent, in huts, motel rooms or glamping tents. Information: *www.lake tekaponz.co.nz*

CHRIST-CHURCH

▨ **MAP INSIDE BACK COVER**
(157 D5) (*ƠƠ F13*) **In minutes, the once beautiful and historic Christchurch was transformed to ruins. 185 people were killed in the powerful earthquake on 22 February 2011, when the entire centre around the main *Cathedral Square* more or less collapsed.** The city is still a construction site, as the repair works in the biggest city on South Island (pop. 380,000) continue at a slow pace due to the astronomic costs. South Islanders are generally stubborn and are very resilient. In recent years, a kind of earthquake tourism has developed. Kim McDonald offers a two-hour INSIDER TIP *Rebuild Walking Tour (from NZ$100 for 2 people | kimsworld.co.nz)*. You explore the historic ruins and learn about the reconstruction effort. If you look beyond the depressed inner city, in Christchurch's suburbs you find fascinating and

🏙 **WHERE TO TO START?**
Arts Centre: The historic building, which has almost been fully refurbished, is in a central position on Worcester Boulevard. From here, you can easily walk to most attractions in the city centre. A small, old-fashioned *Hop-on-Hop-off Tram* makes a circuit once around the city centre. Most buses start from the Bus Interchange *(Lichfield/corner of Colombo Street)* in all directions incl. the airport.

contrasting landscapes: long, wild sandy beaches on the east coast and the bustling *Lyttelton Harbour* at the heart of a green volcanic crater. In the west are the never-ending Canterbury Plains, which are crossed by rivers swelled by melting snow, and behind are the majestic white summits of the South Alps.

SIGHTSEEING

185 WHITE CHAIRS

The empty white chairs created by artist Peter Majendie are a solemn memorial to the 185 earthquake victims. As of the time of press, it was unclear whether the installation will be relocated or finally dismantled. *Cashel/corner of Madras Street*

ARTS CENTRE

Since the reopening in May 2019 life is slowly returning to the arts centre. The Neo-Gothic building, formerly Canterbury University, was severely damaged by the earthquake in 2011, but is now expertly reconstructed. The restaurant, galleries and artisan workshops attract visitors again, and at the markets and outdoor concerts you can get a sense of the spirit to rebuild even better than before. *Daily 10am–5pm | 2 Worcester Blvd. | www.artscentre.org.nz*

CHRISTCHURCH CATHEDRAL

Even in its ruined state, the Cathedral, dating from 1864, is still a city landmark and tourist magnet. The Neo-Gothic, destroyed church on *Cathedral Square* is an impressive monument to the devastating force of the 2011 earthquake. Rebuilding will cost over NZ$104 million. Only five minutes away on foot, as a contrast, is the cardboard reconstruction of the *Transitional Cathedral (daily 8.30am–5pm | 234 Hereford Street | cardboardcathedral.org.nz)*.

INTERNATIONAL ANTARCTIC CENTRE ●

Here, things get uncomfortable – in a simulated Antarctic storm at minus 18 degrees, you experience close up what the New Zealand researchers in the Antarctic have to endure, as well as plenty more about the South Pole. It's cute to watch feeding time for the funny little blue penguins. *Daily 9am–5.30pm | from NZ$59 | 38 Orchard Road | www.iceberg.co.nz*

QUAKE CITY

Interesting, multimedia exhibition at the *Canterbury Museum* about the earthquake and its consequences. *Daily 10am–5pm | admission NZ$20 | 299 Durham Street North/corner of Armagh Street | www.canterburymuseum.com*

FOOD & DRINK

A little hidden away, but in a central location, three restaurants share a canopied outdoor area in *Lichfield Street 89*. There are burgers and fries at *Lower 9th (daily from noon | tel. 03 3 65 73 12 | www.lower9th.co.nz | Budget)*. It's a little classier next door at *Orleans (daily from noon | tel. 03 3 65 73 12 | www.orleans.co.nz |*

A city hub celebrating culture: the Arts Centre

Harbour entrance at Akaroa, French flair down under, with a picturesque small lighthouse

Budget–Moderate), with cocktails and South American dishes, and live music at weekends. And for a sundowner you can head to the rustic bar *Strange & Co. (daily from noon | www.strangeand.co)*.

C1 🌱

Cult café, where mouthwatering burger creations – *sliders* – are literally shot through high pressure hoses from the kitchen into the bar. Vegetarians and allergy-sufferers are also catered for. C1 supports sustainable projects in Samoa and roasts its own coffee. *Daily 7am–10pm | Tuam/corner of High Street | c1es presso.co.nz | Budget*

WHERE TO STAY

BREAKFREE ON CASHEL
Practical, compact, good. Various room options with or without windows. An un-attractive block, but in a central location and a great traveller meeting point. Free Wifi, restaurant, bar and car park (charges apply). *254 rooms | 165 Cashel Street | tel. 03 360 10 64 | www.breakfreeon cashel.nz | Budget–Moderate*

PEGASUS BAY VIEW B&B 🌿
15 minutes from the centre overlooking the sea and near the pleasant suburb of Sumner. Owners Denise and Bernie really look after their guests. *1 room | 121a Moncks Spur Road | tel. 03 384 29 23 | pegasusbayview.co.nz | Moderate*

INFORMATION

CHRISTCHURCH I-SITE
28 Worcester Blvd. | in the Arts Centre | tel. 0800 42 37 83 | www.christchurchnz.com

WHERE TO GO

BANKS PENINSULA (157 D6) (*🝙 G13*)
The 80 km/49.7 mi drive to the green

volcanic peninsula is already a feast for the eyes. In 1840, the French attempted to fight with the British over New Zealand on the peninsula. However, it was five days too late, as Waitangi Treaty had already been signed. But the motto is still "Vive la France!" in the attractive harbour town of *Akaroa (akaroa.com)*. This Francophile atmosphere is effectively exploited for tourists with the appropriate street names, baguettes and the annual *Frenchfest* in October. The mosaic garden in the quaint *Giant's House (Oct–Dec daily noon–4pm, Jan–April noon–5pm, May–Sept 11am–2pm | NZ$20 | 68 Rue Balguerie | thegiantshouse.co.nz | with B&B | Expensive)* is bright and cheerful and was created by the extravagant artist Josie Martin. Tip: it's best to avoid the garden on days when cruise ships have arrived in town. A good alternative is a hike over the crater rims of old volcanos, where sheep now graze on the green hillsides, as far as ☼ *Stony Bay Peak*. Pleasant swimming beaches are in *Okains Bay* with a camp site and shop. The protected natural harbour of Akaroa is teeming with rare sea creatures – like the tiny Hector's dolphins, which can even swim alongside, or which you can watch during the *Black Cat Cruises (Akaroa Main Wharf | several tours daily: swimming NZ$160, animal watch NZ$89 | tel. 0800 93 79 46 | blackcat.co.nz)*.

KAIKOURA ★ (157 E4) (*∅ G12*)

The giant fin of a humpback whale glides majestically into the depths. Orcas, black dolphins and seabirds complete the ocean spectacle against a backdrop of snow-covered mountains in the Kaikoura Range. Breathtaking! New Zealand's whale-watching mecca is a magnet for sea creatures because deep in Kaikoura Canyon warm, subtropical water meets cold, Antarctic sea, which produces a nutrient-rich "superfood" mix.

Even the massive sperm whale has plenty to eat here. It can turn stormy, so it's best to go out on the water during the morning with *Whale Watch Kaikoura (daily several tours | from NZ$180 | Whaleway Station Road | tel. 0800 65 51 21 | www.whalewatch.co.nz)*. You will never forget the sight of a whale from a helicopter: INSIDER TIP whale-watching from the sky is available with *Kaikoura Helicopters (tel. 0800 4 55 43 54 | worldofwhales.co.nz)*. At *Dolphin Encounter (96 Esplanade | tel. 0800 73 33 65 | www.dolphinencounter.co.nz)* there are several daily tours: swimming with dolphins from NZ$175, albatross tours from NZ$125. If you prefer to get active yourself, then book a sunset kayak tour or get close to the inhabitants of the local seal colony by joining a pedal-kayak tour with *Seal Kayak Kaikoura (daily | from NZ$80 | 2 Beach Road | tel. 0800 3 87 73 25 | www.sealkayakkaik oura.com)*.

The strong earthquake in 2016 cut off the small town of Kaikoura (pop. 2,000) for a long while. The ocean floor was raised by several metres, which had an effect on the eco-system. The whales and tourists have now returned. Kaikoura is Maori and means "langoustine meal". You can enjoy large portions five minutes from the centre at the ☼ *Pier Hotel (1 Avoca Street | tel. 03 3 19 50 37 | thepierhotel.co.nz | Budget–Moderate)* with mountain views. Practical accommodation is available at *Bay Cottages (5 rooms | 29a South Bay Parade | tel. 03 3 19 71 65 | baycottages.co.nz | Budget–Moderate)*. More restaurants and cafés are along the esplanade. Information: *Kaikoura i-Site (West End | tel. 03 3 19 56 41 | www.kaikoura.co.nz)*

LYTTELTON HARBOUR
(157 D5) (*∅ F13*)

In Lyttelton Harbour, 12 km/7.5 mi heading south-east, you can spend a delightful half day. The harbour is in a volcanic crater, surrounded by the 446 m/1,463 ft high ☀ *Port Hills*. From the summit you have a view filled with contrasts: in the west, the snow-covered South Alps and Banks Peninsula in the east. The station of the *Christchurch Gondola (daily 10am–5pm | from NZ$28 | 10 Bridle Path Road | Heathcote Valley | www.christchurchat tractions.nz)* is at SH 74 by the road tunnel to Lyttelton.

You can also cycle from Christchurch, as there are plenty of mountain bike routes in Port Hills *(onyourbike.co.nz)*: arrival through Lyttelton Tunnel *(Tunnel Road)* and return through the pleasant bathing locations of *Sumner* and *New Brighton* via the picturesque ☀ Summit and Evans Pass Road. A great restaurant on Sumner beach is *Beach Sumner (daily | 25 Esplanade | tel. 03 3 26 72 26 | www. beachsumner.co.nz | Budget–Moderate)*.

TRANZALPINE EXPRESS ☀

Feet up, keep your eyes open: the train takes about five hours from Christchurch to Greymouth **(156 B4)** *(⚏ E12)* on the west coast – you travel across the sparse Canterbury Plains with deep blue, fast-flowing rivers, over high viaducts and past the impressive *Arthur's Pass* and snow-covered mountain summits. *Daily 8.15am from Christchurch, station in Troup Drive, Addington | 1 hr stop in Greymouth, departs 2.05pm, back in Christchurch 6pm | one way trip from NZ$119 | tel. 0800 87 24 67 | www.greatjourney sofnz.co.nz*

DUNEDIN

🗺 MAP INSIDE BACK COVER
(159 E4) *(⚏ D16)* **Student culture meets colonial architecture: the university city is a mix of magnificent Victorian**

🏙 WHERE TO START?
Octagon: When the locals say: "I'm gonna go into town", they mean George Street with its shops and cafés, which lead to the main Octagon Square, where the roads peel off in all directions. The station, Toitu Otago Settlers Museum and St Paul's Cathedral are a short walk from here. Bus No. 8 travels to St Clair Beach and takes about 30 minutes (bus stops on George Street).

buildings dating from the period of the gold rush and student houses that require refurbishment. The weather in Dunedin (pronounced Dooneedin) is also changeable: on some days, it's high summer in the mornings and autumn in the afternoon. But you should still visit. When the sun comes out in the former Scottish enclave (Dunedin is the old Gaelic name for Edinburgh), it makes the green undulating landscape glisten around New Zealand's old capital city. In summer, the surfers are still riding the waves at St Clair Beach at ten o'clock in the evening and then wax lyrical in the cafés along the promenade about the constant good *swell* in the world's most famous bay for surfers. The water rarely gets warmer than 17 degrees, but it's pleasantly warm in the *Salt Water Pool* in the sea along the cliffs. Occasionally, seals and penguins rest on the rocks around the pool. It's a reminder of how far south you are. You sense that Dunedin is at the bottom of the world where historic buildings are starting to decay because they're no longer required. Then, the city comes alive again: for instance, on Saturdays when the eco-conscious sell their homegrown produce at the 🌐 *Farmer's Market* at the station and bands play between the market stalls. 20,000 students also make the 130,000-strong city come alive where there is a vibrant café culture and live music scene *(dunedinmusic.com)*. The quality of life is high: houses are (still) affordable; the people are super friendly, and you never drive longer than 20 minutes to the next empty beach.

SIGHTSEEING

BALDWIN STREET

Hardened rugby trainers, according to the Guinness Book of Records, let their players run up the steepest street in the world – and even tourists do their best not to get out of breath with a gradient of 35 %. You need about ten minutes to go 350 m/1,148 ft. Fortunately, there's a fountain to drink from at the top.

BOTANIC GARDEN 🌿

Tuis and *bellbirds* twitter in New Zealand's oldest botanical garden among gigantic redwoods and rhododendrons. There are fabulous views of the surroundings. On the meadow in front of the 100-year-old glasshouse, students leaf through their books. At the café *Croque-o-dile* (daily 9.30am–4.30pm) there are croques and crêpes on the menu. *Daily sunrise to sunset | 12 Opoho Road | www.dunedinbotanicgarden. co.nz*

INSIDER TIP ▶ EXPERIENCE DUNEDIN

On a trike for five people, Andrew Sim shows his guests the Otago Peninsula and the best corners of his hometown. With stops at the university, Chinese Gardens and railway station. *60 min/ NZ$65 | tel. 021 2 63 32 61 | www.experiencedunedin.com*

Dunedin's splendid buildings owe their origins to the 19th-century gold rush

It looks like a hall in a noble palace, but it's Dunedin's ... station

OTAGO MUSEUM

Moa skeletons, Maori canoes and Sir Edmund Hillary's passport: the museum on several floors with its own planetarium offers a good insight into New Zealand's history. *Daily 10am–5pm | free admission or for a donation | 419 Great King Street | www.otagomuseum.nz*

RAILWAY STATION

Polite society in long dresses and top hats once paraded around the railway station built in Flemish neo-renaissance style (1907). Today, tourists in colourful outdoor jackets wait for the *Taieri Gorge Railway* (see p. 83), the only train that still departs from here. *Anzac Av.*

TOITU OTAGO SETTLERS MUSEUM ●

What was it like inside the first migrant ships from Europe? How did the Maoris live after their arrival from Polynesia? The 100-year-old museum focuses on visualizing the early beginnings of people settling in Otago. *Daily 10am–5pm | free admission | 31 Queens Garden | www. toituosm.com*

FOOD & DRINK

You should definitely try the local craft beer, freshly caught *blue cod* and gourmet pies from *Who ate all the pies* at the *Farmer's Market (Sat 8am–12.30pm | at the station | www.otagofarmersmarket. org.nz)*. The best cafés and restaurants are at the *Octagon*, in *George Street* and the *Esplanade* at *St Clair Beach*.

THE PERC CAFÉ

Relaxed students froth up milky coffee and balance plates with *eggs benedict* and *seafood chowder* among the tables of this popular café. *Mon–Fri 7am–4pm, Sat/Sun 8am–4pm | 142 Stuart Street | tel. 03 477 5 46 | www.perc.co.nz | Budget*

STARFISH CAFÉ

You visit the café at St Clair Beach for the delicious fish tacos and numerous surfers. Every Friday, different bands play their guitars and drown out the noise of the surf. *Sun–Tue 7am–5pm, Wed–Sat 7am until late | tel. 03 4 55 59 40 | starfishcafe.co.nz | Budget*

VOGEL ST KITCHEN

Where a big graffiti fish decorates the house wall you enter the brick loft with vintage furniture and a display counter filled with delicious food like carrot cake, cheese rolls and beetroot salad. *Mon–Fri 7.30am–3pm, Sat/Sun 8.30am–4pm | 76 Vogel Street | tel. 03 4 77 36 23 | www.vogelstkitchen.nz | Budget*

SHOPPING

GALLERY DE NOVO

Who says that art has to be expensive? Liz Fraser sells photographs, prints, sculptures and paintings in different price categories by young artists from New Zealand. Affordable souvenirs are the cool New Zealand travel posters by Lisa Nicole Moes. *Mon–Fri 9.30am–5.30pm, Sat/Sun 10am–3pm | 101 Stuart Street | www.gallerydenovo.co.nz*

VOID

So, you only packed practical outerwear and want to emanate the cool look of surfers on the beach? In the streetwear shop young relaxed assistants help you choose board shorts, trainers and sunglasses. *Mon–Fri 9am–5.30pm, Sat 10am–5pm, Sun 11am–4pm | 8 Albion Lane | void.co.nz*

LEISURE & SPORTS

BEACHES

Allans Beach is impressive with its craggy cliffs and seals surfing the waves. At *Smails Beach* you either brave the surf or look up from the dunes to the sheep on the high cliffs. To reach *Tunnel Beach*, walk down a steep slope – and you're rewarded with a beach in the middle of high sandstone cliffs.

SURFING

INSIDER TIP *St Clair Beach* has the most reliable surf waves throughout New Zealand. In the wide bay there is a *Surf School (90 min incl. board and neoprene suit NZ$60 | The Esplanade | tel. 0800 48 41 41 | www.espsurfschool.co.nz)* where you can hire the board and there is enough space for beginners to practise.

TAIERI GORGE RAILWAY

In the historic train you travel at a gentle pace through empty countryside – and feel like you're travelling back in time to Otago's past, especially in the 1920s *Heritage Carriages*. Looking through the old wooden windows, you hardly notice any signs of modern life. Instead, there are deep gorges, wild rivers and rugged cliffs. While the train rattles over steep cliffs, you have a bird's eye perspective of the ocean.

The journey from Dunedin to Pukerangi *(159 E4) (D16)* and back takes four hours, including photo stops. From October to April the train departs on Fridays and Sundays and continues to Middlemarch, the starting point of *Otago Central Rail Trail (www.otagorailtrail.co.nz)*. The route heads along disused rail tracks and across viaducts through remote mountain landscapes and old gold-digger towns as far as Clyde in Central Otago. You need about four days for the

230 km/143 mi route. You can take bikes free of charge on the train. *Oct–April daily 9.30am and 2.30pm | Pukerangi return trip NZ$105; single to Middlemarch NZ$78 | tel. 03 4 77 44 49 | www.dunedin railways.co.nz*

ENTERTAINMENT

BREWERIES

Chilli Pils and *Poppy Seed Ale*: the popular micro-brewery *New New New (218 Crawford Street | tel. 03 3 95 64 45 | www.newnewnew.nz)* opens its *tap room* every Friday from 4.30pm–9.30pm. At *Emerson's (daily 10am–10pm | 70 Anzac Av. | tel. 03 4 77 18 12 | emersons.co.nz | Moderate)* there is Indian Pale Ale and stout made in Dunedin. These are tasty in the restaurant with steaks, Merino lamb and freshly caught fish.

INSIDER TIP DOG WITH TWO TAILS ●

Bands test new songs; artists exhibit their works and anyone who wants can spontaneously sit at the piano. The café bar with a small stage, old leather sofas and bookshelves is an experimental showcase for young creative people. *Tue–Sat 8am–midnight, Sun 10am–3pm, Mon 8am–3pm | Moray Place | www.dog withtwotails.co.nz*

INSIDER TIP RIALTO CINEMA ●

An insider tip for rainy days: in the cinema with an Art Deco foyer, it still looks like the 1930s. *11 Moray Place | tel. 03 4 74 22 00 | www.rialto.co.nz*

WHERE TO STAY

DISTINCTION HOTEL

In the 1937 former post office building, the rooms and suites have a sleek executive look. Furnishings are slightly uninspiring, but the rooms are spacious and it's only a few minutes' walk to the Octagon. *121 rooms | 6 Liverpool Street | tel. 03 4 71 85 43 | www.distinctionhotels dunedin.co.nz | Expensive*

ESPLANADE MOTEL

Do you sleep well with the sound of the sea in the background? Then, book one of the ◔ rooms with a kitchenette and ocean view in St Clair. *8 rooms | 14 The Esplanade | tel. 0800 37 72 33 | www.es planade.co.nz | Moderate*

INFORMATION

DUNEDIN I-SITE

50 The Octagon | tel. 03 4 74 33 00 | www. dunedin.govt.nz, www.dunedinnz.com

WHERE TO GO

CATLINS ★

(158–159 C–D5) (∅ C–D 16–17)

Where the wild things are: at sunset, penguins hop out of the sea and seals chase you along the beach. The *Catlins are* 100 km/62 mi south of Dunedin (see p. 127) between Kaka Point and Fortrose. An unspoilt, wind-swept region, where you meet more animals than people. At *Roaring Bay*, you can spot plenty of yellow-eyed penguins *(Information: www.doc.govt.nz),* and at *Nugget Point* you can kayak *(www. catlinskayak.co.nz)* to the seal colony below the lighthouse. Hiking trails lead through the rainforest to the waterfalls like the *Purakaunui* or *Matai Falls*. On the beach at ● *Porpoise Bay*, if you're lucky during the surfing course *(catlins-surf.co.nz)* Hector's dolphins jump with you through the waves, and in *Curio Bay* at low tide a fossilized forest, the *Jurassic Petrified Forest*, is exposed. At Kaka Point, you have the possibility to stay overnight in typical New Zealand

Ancient companions: the 4 m/13.1 ft Moeraki Boulders are about 4 million years old

cribs (kakapointholidayhomes.co.nz), as the locals' holiday houses are called on South Island. From the Eco Retreat *Mohua Park* (see p. 128) in Tawanui, the 3- to 4-hour tours begin with *Catlins Scenic & Wildlife (NZ$150 | tel. 03 4 15 86 13 | catlinsmohuapark.co.nz)*; with local guides you track penguins and seals. Information: *catlins.org.nz, southlandnz.com*

MOERAKI BOULDERS (159 F3) *(⌀ E15)*

Are they alien brains? Or bowls belonging to giants? There are many legends surrounding over 50 round boulders at Koekohe Beach 75 km/46.6 mi north of Dunedin. In fact, they are about 4 million-year-old stones formed by a unique natural phenomenon. According to geologists, up to 2 m/6.6 ft wide megamarbles grow out of the stone on the beach, which is rich in minerals, and was once on the sea bed. You can take some quick photos of the boulders. Afterwards, you should definitely dine in the restaurant *Fleur's Place (Wed–Sun from 9.30am | tel. 03 4 39 44 80 | www. fleursplace.com | Moderate)* in the picture-postcard harbour of *Moeraki*. Fishing boats bring their catch directly to the locals' quay. Chef Fleur Sullivan creates delicious dishes, which have earned her a countrywide reputation, with langoustines, cod and *gurnets*.

OAMARU (159 F3) *(⌀ E15)*

Stranger than fiction: the quiet little town 115 km/71 mi north of Dunedin, which is well known for *little blue penguins* and Victorian architecture, has recently become the world's capital for the steampunk movement. Fans of this subculture wear Victorian costumes and use antiques to make futuristic sculptures or steam-driven companions. The annual *Steampunk Festival* (see p. 19) in May already made it into the Guinness Book of Records thanks to scores of international visitors. The historic centre is a backdrop for the movement, the *Harbour & Tyne Historic Precinct (www.victorianoamaru.co.nz)* with its white limestone Victorian buildings. The *Steam Punk HQ Museum (daily 10am–5pm | NZ$10 | 1 Itchen Street | www.steampunkoamaru.co.nz)* is now here and a playground of the sub-culture in nostalgic style.

One of New Zealand's best craft beers is brewed just around the corner at *Scotts Brewing Co. (daily from 11am | 1 Wansbeck Street | scottsbrewing.co.nz | Budget)* – it has a lovely beer garden and serves crispy stonebaked pizza! At sunset, from here it's a few minutes' walk to the *Little Blue Penguins Colony (evening viewing from 5.30pm, Visitor Center daily from 10am | NZ$15 | 2 Waterfront Road | www.penguins.co.nz)*.

OTAGO PENINSULA (159 E4) (*M E16*)

If you head on Highcliff Road in Dunedin to the peninsula, you constantly want to stop and take photos. From the ✹ crest of the hill you overlook Otago Harbour, green Hobbit hills and cruise ships on the horizon. If you turn right into Seal Point Road, there's another reason to get out your camera: *Yellow Eyed Penguins* on the beach at Sandfly Bay; they usually appear late in the afternoon. It's worth ordering a portion of fish & chips in the historic *1908 Café (Mon/Tue 5pm–8.30pm, Wed–Sun noon–2pm and 5pm–8.30pm | 7 Harington Point Road | tel. 03 4 78 08 01 | www.1908cafe.co.nz | Budget)* in the small coastal town of Portobello, before heading for the world's only *Mainland Colony of Albatrosses (daily from 11.30am to twilight, in winter from 10.30am | NZ$50 | tel. 03 4 78 04 99 | www.albatross.org.nz)*. During a guided tour *(1 hr)* you can watch the rare birds with a wingspan of up to 3.5 m/11 ft through binoculars. You get closer to the animals on a boat tour on the *MV Monarch (1 hr | NZ$54 | www.wildlife.co.nz)*, which stops at Wellers Rock. If you want to explore wildlife on the peninsula with a local expert, you should book a *Cross Country Ride* with the "Peninsula Dundee" aka Perry Reid of *Natures Wonders Otago (1 hr | NZ$99 | tel. 03 4 78 11 50 | www.natureswonders.co.nz)*. The committed nature conservationist takes you to the beaches with penguins and seals in small all-wheel drive vehicles. In the evening, you travel on the winding Portobello Road along the waterfront in Otago Harbour back to Dunedin. Information: *www.otago-peninsula.co.nz*

In 1967 when Barry and Margaret Barker from Wellington purchased ✹ *Larnach Castle (daily 9am–5pm | NZ$31 | 145 Camp Road | www.larnachcastle.co.nz)* on Otago Peninsula 15 km/9.3 mi east of Dunedin, the castle with its panoramic view of Otago Harbour was a ruin.

Today, the former private villa, "New Zealand's unique castle", is a museum. The interior is a reminder of the time when Australian bank manager William Larnach had the building constructed between 1873 and 1886. Four-poster beds made from exotic woods are in the bedrooms and chandeliers hang from the ceiling. As in the old days, every day at 3pm high tea is served in the well-manicured garden (book in advance). In *Larnach Castle Lodge (12 rooms | tel. 03 4 76 16 16 | www.larnachcastle.co.nz | Expensive)* next to the castle you can spend the night in various themed rooms in four-poster beds and old wooden carriages – ✹ many rooms have a bird's eye view of Otago Harbour.

A glacier hiking tour to the fascinating world of Fox Glacier

FRANZ JOSEF

(156 A5) (D13) **Only three glaciers in the world reach as far as the rainforest. Perito Moreno Glacier is in Argentina, while the other two on New Zealand's west coast join with gigantic ice flows and reach inland:** ★ **Franz Josef Glacier and the slightly smaller** *Fox Glacier* **25 km/15.5 mi further south.**

6 km/3.7 mi from the Franz Josef Glacier (named by the geologist Julius von Haast after the Austrian Emperor Franz Josef) is the *Village* nestled between mountain peaks and in the heart of the rainforest. There is plenty of accommodation here and you can book glacier tours with one of the tour operators.

SIGHTSEEING

WEST COAST WILDLIFE CENTRE
Seeing a kiwi in the wild, is like drawing a lucky number in the lottery. *Rowi kiwis* are extremely rare. Only 400 individuals of this species still live in the wild. This breeding station works to ensure their survival. With a *Backstage Kiwi Pass* for NZ$20 on top of the admission price you can even watch how kiwi chicks hatch from the eggs. *Daily 8am–5pm | NZ$38 (pre-book online!) | Cowan/corner of Cron Street | wildkiwi.co.nz*

FOOD & DRINK

SNAKE BITE BREWERY
Asian street food, chocolate cake and craft beer – here, dishes are served that don't necessarily go together, but somehow complement each other. The main thing is the culinary variety in the middle of the rainforest! *Daily 7.30am–10.30pm | 28 Main Road | tel. 03 7 52 02 34 | www. snakebite.co.nz | Budget*

LEISURE & SPORTS

GLACIER TOURS ☌
Take a helicopter to the glacier, e.g. heli tours with *Franz Josef Glacier Guides*

View of the views – when Mount Tasman and Mount Cook are reflected in Lake Matheson

(NZ$460 | www.franzjosefglacier.com), where you fly in a propeller aircraft over the glacier, e.g. sightseeing flights with *Air Safaris* (NZ$370 | airsafaris.co.nz), or hike to the glacier. The tour takes 45 minutes over a rocky riverbed to the viewpoint at the foot of the glacier. The trail begins at a car park five minutes by car from Franz Josef.

GLACIER HOT POOLS

Steaming bathing landscape with several pools in the lush green. Relax in water temperatures between 36 and 40 °C/97 and 104 °F, and afterwards enjoy a massage. *Daily 11am–9pm, no admission after 8pm | Cron Street | tel. 03 752 00 99 | from NZ$28 | www.glacierhotpools.co.nz*

WHERE TO STAY

10 COTTAGES

Light, spacious cottages with kitchen-ettes. You have a view of the rainforest and snow-covered mountains. An ideal starting point for glacier tours. *10 Cottages | 8 Graham Place | tel. 03 752 02 11 | 10cottages.co.nz | Moderate*

RAINFOREST RETREAT

The wooden houses are hidden away in the rainforest and surrounded by snow-covered peaks. Some even have a whirl-pool on the terrace. The dormitories are more reasonably priced at *Flashpackers*, motel rooms and camp sites for camper vans, which also belong to the complex. *22 rooms | 46 Cron Street | tel. 03 752 02 20 | rainforest.nz | Budget–Expensive*

INFORMATION

FRANZ JOSEF I-SITE

63 Cron Street | tel. 0800 35 47 48 | www.glaciercountry.co.nz

wood, stack pebbles on top of each other or gaze at foaming Tasman Sea. Don't forget the sandfly spray!

LAKE MATHESON ☀
(156 A5) (∭ D13)
You will find a very popular photo motif 30 km/18.6 mi south of Franz Josef. In fine weather, Mount Cook and Mount Tasman are reflected here in the "mirror lake" Lake Matheson. Enjoy this view during a 90-minute hike around the lake.

LAKE PARINGA ☀ (159 D1) (∭ C13)
More beautiful than a painting: when the sunshine reflects the surroundings in Lake Paringa, 90 km/55.9 mi south, you will not be able to resist taking photos. The lake is so clear that you can watch the fish on the surface from the canoe. On the lake shore is a *DOC camp site (www.doc.govt.nz)*.

WHERE TO GO

FOX GLACIER ★ ☀
(156 A5) (∭ D13)
The slightly smaller glacier is 25 km/15.5 mi from Franz Josef. You can fly there by helicopter, e.g. with *Fox Glacier Guiding (NZ$450 | www.foxguides.co.nz)*, or walk over rocky boulders on the *Fox Glacier Walk* heading for the icy gorge. The tour *(1 hr)* starts at a car park 2 km/1.2 mi south of *Fox Glacier Township*. On the way, you have to jump across several small streams; at the end is an impressive ☀ viewing platform above the glacier.

INSIDER TIP GILLESPIES BEACH ☀
(156 A5) (∭ D13)
Salty spray flies in your face, and your back is turned on snow-covered summits: 55 km/34.2 mi south-west of Franz Josef, you can build sculptures of drift-

GREYMOUTH

(156 B4) (∭ E12) **In Greymouth, the biggest town on the west coast (pop. 10,000), there were 47 hotels – today, there are only six. Since the wood and coal industry moved away, the building facades are crumbling, and the number of residents is in decline.**

The rather functional town at the mouth of the Grey River is less tourist destination than a starting point for trips along the wild west coast with its wind-swept beaches and towns full of eccentric hippie characters. The coast extends for 500 km/311 mi from Westport in the north to the Haast Pass in the south along the stormy Tasman Sea: a unique mix of rainforests, glaciers, sea and snow-covered summits that almost feels like an illusion.

FOOD & DRINK

MONTEITHS BREWERY

What about culinary delights on the west coast – like *whitebait patties* and Monteiths beer! You can taste both in the brewery's restaurant – and during guided tours *(daily 11.30am, 3pm, 4.30pm & 6pm, NZ$25)* find out all about the history of the 150-year-old beer brand. *Nov–April 11am–9pm, May–Oct 11am–8pm | Turumaha/Herbert Street | tel. 03 7 68 41 49 | thebrewery.co.nz | Budget*

LEISURE & SPORTS

INSIDER TIP GLOWWORM RAFTING

Drift on an old rubber tyre through a canyon in the rainforest and then float along to a cave full of glowworms. Does it sound freaky? It is! But it's incredibly beautiful. The half-day tour with *Wild West Adventures* starts in Greymouth and costs NZ$225. *8 Whall Street | tel. 03 7 68 66 49 | glow-worms. cool*

WEST COAST WILDERNESS TRAIL ⚛

The bike trail leads from Greymouth 139 km/86 mi through rainforests, along secluded lakes and empty beaches filled with driftwood. It's best to book accommodation in advance along the route in *Kumara, Cowboy Paradise (cowboyparadise.co.nz)* and *Hokitika.* The Trail Shuttle Service from *West Coast Wilderness (trailtransport.co.nz)* rents bikes, transports luggage, and collects it en route, if you prefer not to continue along the entire trail.

WHERE TO STAY

OAK LODGE

B & B in an old wooden villa 3 km/1.9 mi outside Greymouth. Generous break-

LORD OF THE RINGS HYPE

New Zealand is the cult destination for Hobbit fans. The *Lord of the Rings* and Hobbit trilogies were filmed in New Zealand. At the film locations, every stone is marketed for its tourism appeal. There are countrywide LOTR tours (Lord of the Rings). You can cross off one dramatic and picturesque location after the next. It's cheaper to design your own tour. The Department of Conversation (DOC) has compiled a list of film locations in conservation areas: *www. doc.govt.nz*. Most of them are around Queenstown. Simply drive up Mount Cardrona for an impressive view of Middle Earth. Straight ahead between the mountains is the shadow mountain valley. In Arrowtown, you follow the trail of Bilbo, Gandalf and the dwarfs along the Arrow River and to the Ford of Bruinen. *Dart River Safaris* (see p. 105) offers tours on the water and on horseback from Glenorchy; *Heli Glenorchy (heliglenorchy.co.nz)* offers aerial tours of the locations. You can get your magic ring in Nelson from *Jens Hansen* (see p. 95). The *Weta Workshop Studios* (see p. 137) in Wellington offers a glimpse behind the scenes of the film prop assistants and animation artists. If you want to take film-ready photos with authentic scenery, then head for the Shire to Hobbiton (see p. 57) near Matamata.

fast, spa pool, sauna and beautiful garden. *5 rooms | 286 State Highway 6 | tel. 03 7 68 68 32 | www.oaklodge.co.nz | Moderate*

GREYMOUTH I-SITE
1 Mackay Street/Herbert Street | tel. 03 7 68 51 01 | westcoast.co.nz

PUNAKAIKI ᪲ (156 B3) (*E11*)
It took a long time to stack all these pancakes on top of each other: the *Pancake Rocks* at Tasman Bay in Punakaiki, 70 km/43.5 mi north of Greymouth are estimated to be about 30 million years old. A magnificent photo backdrop – especially when the spray rushes through the holes in the rocks.
The picturesque *Punakaiki Beach Camp (5 Owen Street | tel. 03 7 31 18 94 | www.punakaikibeachcamp.co.nz | Budget)* is between the beach, rainforest and tall cliffs and has space for camper vans and tents, huts and reasonably priced holiday houses. You can explore more of the wilderness on *Canoe Tours (riverkayaking.co.nz)* on Pororari River.

REEFTON (156 C3) (*F11*)
Have you always wanted to hang out with gold-diggers with beards? Now is your chance in the town (pop. 1,000), 80 km/49.7 mi north-east of Greymouth. 150 years after the gold rush, you still see rugged characters with dirty boots in old gold-digger huts brewing tea in tin billy pots over an open fire. At least, at the INSIDER TIP *Bearded Mining Company (admission for a donation | 37 Walsh Street | tel. 03 732 83 77 | www.reefton.co.nz)* you can learn gold panning.

Greymouth's beer Monteiths is even better today than during the gold rush era

WESTPORT (156 C3) (*E11*)
The sleepy town (pop. 4,000), 85 km/ 52.8 mi north of Greymouth, is the gateway to the secluded northern part of the west coast. 12 km/7.5 mi along the coast is *Tauranga Bay,* a popular meeting point for surfers and seals.
You will feel very remote from everything in the village of *Karamea* with sub-tropical micro-climate between the mountains and sea 90 km/55.9 mi northwards on the edge of Kahurangi National Park. Under Nikau palms in the dense rainforest you can stay overnight in the pleasant *Last Resort (26 rooms| 71 Waverley Street | tel. 03 7 82 66 17 | lastresortkaramea.co.nz | Budget)* with an excellent restaurant. Nearby, there are karst caves and the start of the ᪲ *Heaphy Track,* one of

Classic: spiral-shaped jade charms

New Zealand's Great Walks, in Kahurangi National Park. The warm climate also benefits *Mokihinui*, 50 km/31.1 mi north of Westport. You can camp at the mouth of the Mokihinui Rivers which is excellent for swimming and canoeing. Highly recommended are also the *Beach Cabins (www.gentleannie.co.nz | Budget)* and *Cowshed Café (Budget)* on the camping ground where the wood-fired grill for pizza is fuelled by driftwood from the beach.

HOKITIKA

(156 B4) (*m E12*) **During the gold rush Hokitika was one of New Zealand's densely populated towns. Historic buil-** dings and shops with **Wild West facades are still reminders of this era.**
Today, in the town between the sea and Alps (pop. 4,000) everything is about the "green gold" – jade from the surrounding rivers. Numerous jewellery ateliers in Hokitika make creative pieces with the stone. At the *Wildfoods Festival (wildfoods.co.nz)* in March the number of residents increases threefold when visitors from across the country flock to Hokitika to try bush specialities like worms and deep-fried beetles.

FOOD & DRINK

AURORA RESTAURANT
Fine food for everyone: in the gourmet restaurant, for breakfast there are eggs benedict with homemade Hollandaise sauce, pulled-pork burgers for lunch, tapas in the afternoon and freshly caught fish in the evening. *Tue–Sun 8am–9.30pm (closed in winter) | 19 Tancred Street | tel. 03 755 83 19 | aurora hoki.co.nz | Moderate*

SHOPPING

BONZ 'N' STONZ
Design your own necklace charms from jade or bone and create under expert instruction. The courses last three to six hours and cost between NZ\$90 and 180. *Daily 9am–5pm | 16 Hamilton Street | tel. 03 755 65 04 | Facebook: bonznstonz*

TECTONIC JADE
Charms and artworks from especially rare jade stones, made using traditional methods. Each amulet has a different meaning and, according to the owner Rex Scott, is not made from stone but "tears of the earth". *Daily 8.30am–5pm | 67 Revell Street | tel. 03 755 66 44 | www. tectonicjade.com*

ENTERTAINMENT

REGENT THEATRE ●
In case it should rain (which happens frequently on the west coast), then visit this beautiful old cinema with red cushioned seats in an Art Deco building from 1935. *Daily | 23 Weld Street | tel. 03 755 81 01 | hokitikaregent.com*

WOODSTOCK HOTEL
The first gold-diggers already got drunk in the pub and hotel from 1870. Nowadays, regular live bands perform here. At the jam session on Sunday everyone is allowed on stage – locals and tourists. The view from the 🍃 beer garden over the mountains and rivers is spectacular. You should definitely try the *whitebait* omelet! *Daily from 4pm | 250 Woodstock Rimu Road | tel. 03 755 89 09 | www.woodstockhotel.net | Budget*

WHERE TO STAY

TEICHELMANNS
B & B in a historic timber house in the old gold-digger district. Beautiful antiques and light rooms. The perfect location to immerse yourself in Eleanor Catton's book "The Luminaries" that is set during the gold rush in Hokitika. *6 rooms | 20 Hamilton Street | tel. 03 755 82 32 | teichelmanns.nz | Moderate*

INFORMATION

HOKITIKA I-SITE
Weld Street/Railway Terrace | at the Clock Tower | tel. 03 755 61 66 | hokitika.org

WHERE TO GO

HOKITIKA GORGE (156 B4) (*🛍 E12*)
Has someone helped with photoshop? No, the water in the glacial river

35 km/21.8 mi south is really as turquoise as on the photos! Make up your own mind: from the car park it's a 15-minute walk to the rope bridge over the gorge. Unfortunately, there are lots of sandflies.

LAKE MAHINAPUA (156 B4) (*🛍 E12*)
At last, a lake on the west coast where you don't shiver with cold. Jump from the long boardwalk into the water, which is a pleasant temperature, and swim towards the snow-covered Alps in the distance! It's worth spending a night on the *DOC Camp Site (www.doc.govt.nz)* by the lakeside purely because of the fiery red sunsets. About 10 km/6.2 mi south of Hokitika.

ROSS (156 B4) (*🛍 E12*)
The biggest gold nugget that was ever found in New Zealand (2.8 kg/6.2 lbs!) was from Ross 30 km/18.6 mi south-

LOW BUDGET

Groups of up to six people can visit the Rippon Vineyard free of charge (pre-booking not necessary) *(daily 11am–5pm | 246 Wanaka-Mt. Aspiring Road | tel. 03 4 43 80 84 | www.rippon.co.nz)* on Lake Wanaka. Plus, you can taste Sauvignon Blancs and Pinot Noirs. However, the owners appreciate a small donation.

28 wall murals by street art artists from around the world decorate the centre of Dunedin. You can explore the free open-air museum with the help of the *Dunedin Street Art Map (online at dunedinstreetart.co.nz).* The tour lasts about 90 minutes.

Roses and life artists flourish in the mild climate of Nelson

west of Hokitika. It's an incentive to borrow the gold-digger tools at the *Ross Goldfields Information & Heritage Centre (4 Aylmer Street | tel. 03 755 40 77 | www.rossgoldtown.org)* and try your luck at Jones Creek.

NELSON

(157 E2) *(ᗕ G10)* **A small town with big ideas. In Nelson (pop. 50,000) you can explore the cultural landscape between Abel Tasman National Park and Marlborough Sounds.**

About 400 artists live in the town which boasts the country's longest hours of sunshine. They exhibit their works in museums and galleries, e.g. *The Suter*

Art Gallery (daily 9.30am–4.30pm | free admission | 208 Bridge Street | thesuter. org.nz). The *Wow Museum* shows cool "art on the body". What else? There are plenty of beautiful old wooden villas and regular markets.

NATIONAL WOW MUSEUM

It's retro and future-oriented: the museum displays old-timers and "portable art" that looks as if the Iceland singer and performance-art artist Björk commissioned the Wow to design stage outfits for her. Every year new pieces are added from the design competition "World of Wearable Art" (WOW) in Wellington. Every September, fashion and costume designers from around the world can test their creative talents. *Daily 10am–5pm | NZ$24 | 95 Quarantine Road | www.wowcars.co.nz*

PARKER GALLERY

Kiwi art: paintings, sculptures, jewellery and photography by artists from Nelson and the vicinity. *Mon–Fri 9.30am–4.30pm, Sat 10am–4pm | 90 Achilles Av.*

FOOD & DRINK

INSIDER TIP THE KITCHEN ⊘

Superfood smoothies, halloumi salad and organic cappuccinos: in the bright restaurant with purist furniture it's all about *positive eating*. All ingredients come from the region and are 100 % organic. There are vegan banana waffles with raspberry chia jam for breakfast and quinoa salads or paleo burgers with manuka bacon and organic beef for lunch. *Mon–Fri 8am–3pm, Sat until 2pm | 111 Bridge Street | tel. 021 195 82 46 | ktchn.co.nz | Expensive*

SHOPPING

JENS HANSEN

There it is – the ring everyone is looking for! Jens Hansen, a Danish-born jewellery designer, created the famous magic ring from "The Lord of the Rings". After his death, his son continues his business and also sells models, which were inspired by actors from the film: "The Ring for Viggo" or "The Ring for Cate". *Mon–Fri 9am–5pm, Sat 9am–2pm | 320 Trafalgar Square | www.jenshansen.com*

MARKETS

Every Wednesday at the ⊘ *Farmer's Market (8am–2pm | Maitai Blvd.)* there are fresh figs and apples from the vicinity. Live bands perform. On Saturdays, people meet at *Nelson Market (8am–*

1pm) between artisan products and nectarines from the region at *Montgomery Square* and on Sundays at the *Flea Market (8am–1pm)* at the same location.

LEISURE & SPORTS

SWIMMING

The best swimming locations are on the city outskirts at *Tahunanui Beach* or on *Rabbit Island* with *glamping sites (from SH 60, turn off to Upper Moutere | www.applebyhouse.co.nz)*.

ENTERTAINMENT

THE WORKSHOP

A café, bar and micro-brewery in an old workshop. The bar is in an old ship's container with a car on the roof. Alternative rock bands, swing dance evenings and draught craft beer. Tasty snacks are burgers, steaks and fish dishes. *Wed–Sun 3pm–11pm | 32c New Street | tel. 021 55 61 58 | Budget*

WHERE TO STAY

JOYA GARDEN & VILLA STUDIOS ⊘

B & B with double rooms and studios in the garden of an historic villa. Organic breakfast (on request, also vegetarian or vegan) with ingredients from the garden. ☆ Terrace with views over Nelson. *4 rooms | 49 Brougham Street | tel. 03 5 39 13 50 | www.joya.co.nz | Moderate*

WAKEFIELD QUAY HOUSE

B & B in a listed colonial villa from 1905. At sunset the owner Woodi Weine serves meals on the ☆ wooden veranda with a view of Tasman Bay. Breakfast and drinks in the evening are included in the price. *2 rooms | 385 Wakefield Quay | tel. 03 5 46 72 75 | www.wakefieldquay.co.nz | Expensive*

NELSON I-SITE
77 Trafalgar Street | tel. 03 5 48 23 05 | www.nelsontasman.nz

WHERE TO GO

ABEL TASMAN NATIONAL PARK ★
(157 D1) (*ШШ G10*)

Turquoise gleaming water and the right temperature for swimming (!) and golden beaches, nestled in thick vegetation – no wonder that New Zealand's smallest national park 80 km/49.7 mi north-west of Nelson attracts crowds of visitors. A good starting point is the INSIDER TIP *camp site at Totaranui (end Dec–start Feb at least 3 days | book online at www. doc.govt.nz | Budget)* at the north end of the national park. After sunset, the only light is from the moon and torches. Conversations with the camping neighbours revolve around the size of the fish that were caught by the cliffs during the day. What can be more idyllic? On the *Abel Tasman Coastal Track*, which leads 60 km/37.3 mi from Totaranui to Marahau, you can hike in 4–5 days from one dream beach to the next. Or enjoy a comfortable ride in the *water taxi (approx. NZ$49 | tel. 03 5 27 80 83 | www.aqua taxi.co.nz)* and ask to stop a beach of your choice and be collected in the evening. From *Torrent Bay* half-way along the route a path leads to the cliff pool with emerald green water in the rainforest. On a 10 m/33 ft long rockslide, you can slide into INSIDER TIP *Cleopatra's Pool*. At the southern park end in Marahau you will find *The Barn (160 beds | 14 Harvey Road | tel. 03 5 27 80 43 | www. barn.co.nz | Budget)* with huts in a pleasant location and reasonably priced dormitories. If you prefer not to go hiking: *Marahau Sea Kayaks (kayak for 2 people* approx. NZ$170/day | 10 Franklin Street | tel. 0800 52 92 57 | www.msk.co.nz)* hires kayaks for trips along the coast and organizes one- or multi-day tours with a guide. Information: *Abel Tasman i-Site (20 Wallace Street | Motueka | tel. 03 5 28 65 43 | www.motuekaisite.co.nz)*.

GOLDEN BAY (157 D1) (*ШШ F–G 9–10*)

At the end things turn out beautifully: the ≋≋ *Farewell Spit* in the far north-west (170 km/106 mi from Nelson) is South Island's happy ending. The narrow headland measures 35 km/21.8 mi and embraces Golden Bay from the left. 4 km/2.5 mi are open to the public, while the rest of the nature reserve is filled with migratory birds, sea lions and wind-swept dunes that are only accessible as part of guided tours, e.g. with ◉ *Farewell Spit Eco Tours (7 hr/ NZ$155,| www.farewellspit.com)*.

Also fabulous is a horse ride through the salty spray at Puponga Beach at the foot of Farewell Spit – tours for beginners with *Cape Farewell Horse Treks (1.5 hr/ NZ$80,| horsetreksnz.co.nz)*. The best swimming beaches in Golden Bay are *Pohara, Tata Beach* and *Totaranui* at the start of the Abel Tasman National Park. ≋≋ *Whara-riki Beach* is not suitable for swimming, but it's dramatic and beautiful and located on the west coast near Puponga *(20 min on foot from the car park)* with waves splashing around cliff arches out in the sea. On the *Wainui Falls Track* near Mohua it's a 40-minute walk to a waterfall in the rainforest. At INSIDER TIP *The Mussel Inn (musselinn.co.nz)* between the hippie towns of Collingwood and Takaka, in the middle of nowhere, perhaps you will experience the party night of your life. Musicians from all over New Zealand perform in the rustic hut with disco ball on the ceiling in the small coastal community of Onekaka. A rebellious café, which has already been brewing its own beer since the 1990s *(Pale Whale Ale)*, organizes open-mike evenings and serves fresh seafood (you should definitely try the Green Lipped Mussels!). It's a short walk to *Laidback Lodge (3 rooms | 23 Iron Works Road |*

Kahurangi, New Zealand's second largest national park (after Fiordland) to the east of Nelson is known as "valuable treasure" in Maori dialect, because it leads to the west coast with its many rivers filled with *Pounamu* (greenstone). The song of tuis and bellbirds fills the air and occasionally

On horseback, the dream setting on Wharariki Beach looks almost extra-terrestrial

tel. 03 5 25 62 44 | laidbacklodge.co.nz | Moderate), where you can sleep in wooden huts or in a retro caravan in the bush. You can also walk to the *Moonbow B&B (2 rooms | 1430 Takaka-Collingwood Highway | tel. 03 5 25 92 98 | www.moon bowbeach.co.nz | Moderate)* on the beach at Tukurua.

KAHURANGI NATIONAL PARK
(156–157 C–D 1–2) (*ω F10*)
The *Heaphy Track*, one of New Zealand's Great Walks, continues for 78 km/ 48.5 mi through sub-tropical rainforest, river valleys and secluded beaches. The

large kiwis rustle in the bush. If you feel confident: in *Mount Owen* there is a labyrinthine cave system. *www.doc.govt.nz*

NELSON LAKES NATIONAL PARK
(157 D3) (*ω F–G11*)
Here, glaciers were at work and shaped the unique landscape with steep mountains and large lakes 88 km/54.7 mi south of Nelson. A good starting point for hikes is the village *St Arnaud* on Lake Rotoiti. If you are a keen angler, the lakes in the park are full of trout. The nearby *Rainbow Ski Field* is open from June to October.

PICTON

(157 E–F2) (⚏ H10) Every time a ferry arrives from North Island, the small town with a population of 3,000, on Queen Charlotte Sound comes to life. Then, restaurants and cafés on the waterfront fill up as well as the tour operator shops which organize trips to Marlborough Sounds.

With glistening green water and beautiful historic buildings: you should stay a night and taste the fresh fish in the numerous excellent restaurants. Or hike on the *Tirohanga Track (45 min)* directly on the harbour to a ⋇ viewpoint with a fabulous view over the Sounds. If you want to travel further: ⋇ *Queen Charlotte Drive* heads from Picton on a winding road for 40 km/24.9 mi to Havelock and past tranquil bays. You should definitely stop at the ⋇ *lookout* at *Cullens Point,* and use up your storage with countless photos of the fjord!

FOOD & DRINK

LE CAFÉ 🟢 ⋇
A wonderful way to consume calories: lamb- and fish dishes with views of the gleaming green of Queen Charlotte Sound. Organic ingredients that are locally grown, tasty beer and regular live music. *Daily 7am–midnight| 12–14 London Quay | tel. 03 5 73 55 88 | www.lecafepicton.co.nz | Budget*

LEISURE & SPORTS

BOAT TOURS
What about a kayak tour through the tranquil water of Queen Charlotte Sound? A 3.5 hr tour with the *Marlborough Sounds Adventure Company (tel. 03 573 60 78 | marlboroughsounds.co.nz)*

costs approx. NZ$95. Or do you prefer a *Gourmet Cruise (NZ$125 | tel. 0800 50 40 90 | www.cougarline.co.nz)* to *Raeti Lodge* (green lipped mussels!) in the dense vegetation on the shore of Kenepuru Sound?

INSIDER TIP ▶ SAILING
Cast off for the past: on the *Steadfast*, a reconstruction of a French sailing cutter of 1913, you can glide noiselessly through Queen Charlotte Sound. *6 hr/NZ$180 incl. food | tel. 03 5 76 52 98 | www.steadfastsail.co.nz*

HIKING
The popular ⋇ *Queen Charlotte Track* winds 70 km/43.5 mi through the bush and over mountains with views of jade-green fjords. The tour lasts for 4–5 days. But from Picton you can also ask to leave the boat and carry on walking on the track for this part of the route, e.g. a *1 day guided walk* from Picton with *Wilderness Guides (NZ$365 | tel. 03 5 73 54 32 | www.wildernessguidesnz.com)*.

WHERE TO STAY

BEACHCOMBER INN ⋇
Arrive by ferry and check in on the waterfront: the rooms at the Beachcomber Inn are slightly impersonal, but the view over the harbour more than compensates. *35 rooms | 27 Waikawa Road | tel. 03 5 73 89 00 | pictonhotel.com | Moderate*

SENNEN HOUSE
Beautiful old world: a white colonial villa with palm garden 15 minutes' walk from the ferry quay. Apartments with antique beds and shelves and a kitchenette. *4 rooms | 9 Oxford Street | tel. 03 5 73 52 16 | www.sennenhouse.co.nz | Expensive*

Wake up! The ferry is coming! Picton springs to life to the rhythm of the ferry timetable

INFORMATION

PICTON I-SITE
The Foreshore | Tel. 03 5 20 3113 | marl boroughnz.com

WHERE TO GO

BLENHEIM (157 E2) *(M H10–11)*
So, you're not into wines and never wanted to become a connoisseur? Beware, when you arrive at Blenheim, 28 km/17.4 mi south of Picton. Around the small town is New Zealand's biggest wine-growing region *Marlborough* (75 % of all NZ wines come from here). There is a high chance that you will soon be sniffing fine vintages in wine goblets. The region's prizewinning Sauvignon Blancs simply taste too good – especially if you drink a glass of *Cloudy Bay* on the beach in *Cloudy Bay* or treat yourself to some wines from the winery *Hans Herzog* (*81 Jeffries Road | www.herzog.co.nz*): the

vines grow on the hillsides around the estate. On the *Wine Tours by Bike (from Renwick | tel. 03 5 72 79 54 | www.wine toursbybike.co.nz)* you can travel from one estate to the next (hopefully, not in wiggly lines!), or discover new varieties by driving along the *Marlborough Wine Trail (www.wine-marlborough.co.nz)*. A feast for the taste buds is lunch at the winery *Wairau River (daily noon–3pm | 11 Rapaura Road | wairauriverwines.com | Moderate)*. Here, you can savour the region's many delicacies (e.g. salmon and prawns).

INSIDER TIP ⯈ CAPE CAMPBELL ☆
(154 C5) *(M H11)*
Solitary point: the 100-year-old *lighthouse* on a rock spur in the sea played the starring role in the Hollywood film "The Light Between Oceans" alongside Michael Fassbender and Alicia Vikander. The black-and-white circled building is on the white cliffs of Clifford Bay in

total seclusion, 80 km/49.7 mi southeast of Picton. The only living creatures that you meet here are fur seals on the beach. At the foot of the lighthouse you can spend the night in the *cottage (NZ$150/night | 505 Cape Campbell Road | Seddon | tel. 021 183 90 61 | experiencecapecampbell.co.nz)* from the film setting with a wooden veranda – it's incredibly romantic!

INSIDER TIP D'URVILLE ISLAND
(157 E1) (*Ø G–H10*)
It doesn't get more remote: on D'Urville Island at the northern end of Marlborough Sounds only 52 people live on the same site, which is bigger than the Island of Jersey. Arriving here is an adventure, but it's worth it. From Okiwi Bay (55 km/34.2 mi from Havelock), it's about an hour's drive on a gravel road with a film-set vista over the green cliffs and sea. At the end of the road is the *French Pass*, where giant whirlpools are regularly formed in the sea by the tides. You can take a small car ferry from here *(tel. 03 576 53 30 | durvillecrossings.co.nz)* to the other side in 15 minutes. The few fishermen and nature conservationists, who live on D'Urville Island, will be delighted with your visit and keen to tell you where you can fish for the best blue cod and snappers, and which hikes are worthwhile through the wilderness. In the *Wilderness Resort (6 rooms | Rural Bag 1211 Rai Valley | tel. 03 576 52 68 | durvilleisland.co.nz | Moderate)* you can stay overnight in wooden huts on the beach. *Driftwood Eco Tours (driftwoodecotours.co.nz)* offers multi-day trips incl. the journey here.

MARLBOROUGH SOUNDS ★
(157 E–F 1–2) (*Ø G–H10*)
50 Shades of Green: the clear water gleams like polished jade and the shore is covered with the dark green rainforest. Houses stand boldly on rock spurs in the chirping vegetation and on the shore there are scores of small hidden bays. 20 per cent of New Zealand's (!) coastline is in Marlborough Sounds – there's plenty to discover in this fjord landscape, which according to Maori legend was raised by the tentacles of a giant octopus. There are flooded valleys where dolphins swim and green lipped mussels grow. If you are camping or caravanning, e.g. along the *Kenepuru Sound* there are lots of small beaches for camping. *Cowshed Bay, Nikau Cove* and *Picnic Bay* are particularly attractive. This is somewhere you can forget time – ● INSIDER TIP *Nydia Bay Lodge (24 beds | tel. 03 579 84 11 | www.onthetracklodge.nz | Moderate)*, where you can sleep in wooden chalets, Mongolian yurts or in an old train carriage. It's best to be dropped off here by the *Pelorus Sound Mailboat (1.5 hr from Havelock | tel. 03 574 10 88 | themailboat.co.nz)* and spend several days kayaking, snorkelling and hiking along the *Nydia Track*.

QUEENS-TOWN

(158 C3) (*Ø C15*) **It's best to visit the waterfront first where everything is concentrated in a central location in** ★ **Queenstown: adventure sports enthusiasts, buskers, flirting backpackers and a spectacular setting in nature.**
Lake Wakatipu sparkles light blue and the jagged cliffs of the Remarkables mountain range give the unique scenery its dramatic quality. You instantly feel compelled to see and do lots of things. Bungy jumping, parachuting or ride in a speedboat first? In the "world's adventure capital", it's difficult to decide what

thrilling activities you should do first. You can escape the hustle and bustle on the T.S.S. Earnslaw, a 1912 steamer, which departs at a more relaxed pace from the *line.co.nz*) over a winding racing track or with a *tandem paragliding fight (NZ$239 | tel. 0800 75 96 88 | www.nzgforce.com)*. If you make the ascent after dark, you can

Only one of many ways to feel the adrenalin rush in Queenstown: bungy jumping

waterfront several times daily. Out on the lake you can admire the nature which is truly breathtaking.

admire the countless stars of the southern hemisphere and enjoy some *stargazing (NZ$99 incl. gondola ride | from Skyline Gondola Station Brecon Street | www.skyline.co.nz)*.

SIGHTSEEING

BOB'S PEAK ☆

Your sights are set on the panoramic vista of Lake Wakatipu at an altitude of 450 m/1,476 ft – 60 minutes on the Tiki Trail. Or you can take the *cable car (start Brecon Street)* up the mountain. At the summit, hiking trails and 12 different mountain bike tracks invite you to explore the great outdoors. But it's also fine to sit in the *Skyline Café* and enjoy the views of Coronet Peak and the Remarkables. You can make the descent in a bobsled *The Luge (NZ$55 | tel. 03 441 01 01 | www.sky*

GIBBSTON VALLEY WINE

So, you think wine tasting is elitist and boring? This vineyard will surprise you. There are no wine snobs anywhere – instead, there is a party atmosphere amidst the green hills. The restaurant hosts stag parties and several thousand visitors attend the annual summer concert with international stars in January. You must try the cheese from the in-house dairy! *Daily 10am–5pm | 1820 State Highway 6 | tel. 03 442 69 10 | www.gibbstonvalley nz.com*

Bungy is not enough? Then speed in a jet boat across Shotover River

FOOD & DRINK

INSIDER TIP THE BESPOKE KITCHEN

In the bright restaurant, which is popular with young people from around the world, the food tastes as good as it looks (muesli with floral deco!). It's also super healthy, as the ingredients for the halloumi burgers and smoothie bowls are from organic farms in the region. On the ☼ terrace, you feel far away from the busy crowds on the waterfront. *Daily 8am–5pm | 9 Isle Street | tel. 03 4 09 05 52 | www.bespokekitchen. co.nz | Budget*

THE COW PIZZA

Many restaurants in Queenstown lack atmosphere because they are located in modern buildings. But not here! In the old cow shed, you sit at rustic wooden tables by candlelight and almost feel like you're in a Swiss ski chalet. The mix of pizza, pasta, beer and loud music has been a success for 40 years. *Daily noon–midnight | Cow Lane | tel. 03 4 42 85 88 | thecowpizza.co.nz | Budget*

RATA

Plenty of wood and large paintings of the moss-covered rainforest: in the restaurant run by star chef Josh Emett the guests feel like they are surrounded by nature. Fine New Zealand dishes are served like whitebait ceviche from the west coast, squid from Bluff or mussels from Cloudy Bay. Special tip: try the particularly tender Te Mana lamb from New Zealand's high mountains. *Daily noon–10pm | 43 Ballarat Street | tel. 03 4 42 93 93 | www.rata dining.co.nz | Expensive*

SHOPPING

VESTA

Queenstown's shopping streets are uninspiring with lamb fleece stores and international shopping chain branches. Fortunately, there are exceptions like this original design shop in the oldest cottage in Queenstown that sells art prints, jewellery and lamps made by New Zealand artists. *Mon–Sat 10am–5pm | 19 Marine Parade | www.vestadesign.co.nz*

THE WALK IN WARDROBE

Tourists from around the world take their used clothing to the "preloved fashion boutique". The choice of international brands is particularly large. *Thu–Mon 10am–8.30pm, Tue/Wed until 6pm | Beech Tree Arcade | 34 Shotover Street | www.thewalkinwardrobe.co.nz*

THE WINERY

Try the boutique wines from small wineries in New Zealand, and you can also send your choices back home from here. *Daily 10.30am–10.30pm | 14 Beach Street | www.thewinery.co.nz*

LEISURE & SPORTS

In Queenstown, there are numerous possibilities for adventure – e.g. horizontal bungy jumping. The world's highest human catapult, the ● *Nevis Catapult (NZ$255 | Gibbston | tel. 0800 2 86 49 58 | www.bungy.co.nz)* propels you up to 100 km/h/62 mph at a height of 150 m/492 ft across a gorge. Immediately next to this, you can jump from a height of 134 m/440 ft with your feet secured by a traditional *bungy line (NZ$275 | same provider)* from a cabin over the gorge towards the Nevis River. Free fall for 8.5 seconds! Hydro Attack is the name of a *speed boat (NZ$149 | Beach Street | tel. 27 4 77 90 74 | www.hydroattack.co.nz)* in the shape of a shark which races at 80 km/h/50 mph across the lake, dives under water and finally shoots straight up in the air out of the water like a fish.

In the *Shotover Jet (NZ$149 | tel. 0800 74 68 68 | www.shotoverjet.com)* you speed towards the cliff faces in steep canyons only to avert a collision at the very last minute. The ultimate adrenalin kick are the "awesome foursome" *(information at www.combos.co.nz)*: Nevis bungy, a ride with the Shotover Jet, helicopter flight to Skippers Canyon and rafting on Shotover River for a total of NZ$700 – everything in one day.

Do you feel dizzy when you hear that? Then take things at a more leisurely pace: a fabulous experience of the great outdoors is INSIDERTIP *packrafting (8–10 hr | from NZ$320 | packraftingnz.com)*: with a foldable canoe in a rucksack you trek across the empty *Reese Valley* 45 km/28 mi north of Queenstown and canoe on secluded rivers to an area that is called "paradise" for good reason. Or use the many *mountain-bike trails* around Queenstown. The brochure *Mountain Bike Riding* informs you about the best routes and is available from the Department of Conservation (see p. 104). Mountain bikes, e-Bikes, tandems and trailers for family tours are available for hire from *Cycle Higher (9b Earls Street | tel. 03 4 42 95 59 | www.cyclehigher.com)*.

On the INSIDERTIP *Welcome Rock Trail* 70 km/43.5 mi south of Queenstown, you cycle on private land away from the crowds and through the mountains. On the way, you can stay overnight in one of the old *gold-digger huts (from NZ$130/night | tel. 27 2 39 26 28 | www.welcomerock.co.nz)*. When it snows from June/July, Queenstown's ski regions *Coronet Peak* and *The Remarkables* open for about three months.

ONSEN HOT POOLS ● ≈

The view of the mountains is even more enjoyable if you're surrounded by warm bubbles. The wooden tubs filled with mountain water are on the cliffs above Shotover River and are divided from each other by wooden partition walls. You can book each pool for up to four people. *Daily 9am–11pm | NZ$75 | 160 Arthurs Point Road | tel. 03 442 57 07 | www.onsen.co.nz*

T. S. S. EARNSLAW ●

The 1912 vintage steamer is part of Queenstown like the Eiffel Tower in Paris. Six times daily the "Lady of the Lake" with smoking funnel departs on a 1.5-hour tour of Lake Wakatipu. If you want, you can get off at the *Walter Peak Station* and watch one of the sheep-shearing shows here – or enjoy horse-riding (40-minute tour with guide) in the great outdoors. The tour company is *Real Journeys (from NZ$70 | Steamer Wharf/ 88 Beach Street | tel. 0800 65 65 01 | www.realjourneys.co.nz)*.

ENTERTAINMENT

ATLAS BEER CAFE ☲

The bar is small, but there is a wide choice of craft beer. Try unusual beers like *Yeastie Boyz* or *Parrot Dog*, and enjoy a drink at the bar with the many locals. With a lake view! *Daily 10am–2pm | 88 Beach Street | atlasbeercafe.com*

THE LODGE BAR

A lake view, selected wines and interiors like in a luxury hunting lodge. In the bar of the New Zealand outdoor label Rodd & Gunn meat pies and oysters are served with Pinot Noir and Sauvignon Blanc. Sometimes, it's nice to be enjoy a touch of class! *Mon–Thu from 4pm, Fri–Sun from noon | 2 Rees Street | www.roddand gunn.com*

WHERE TO STAY

LAKESIDE MOTEL ☲

At last, accommodation in Queenstown with a lake view that doesn't charge

extortionate prices. A central location, studios with kitchen facilities, free parking and a dream setting through the window – what more do you want? *7 rooms | 18 Lake Esplanade | tel. 03 4 41 88 00 | www.lakesidemotel.co.nz | Moderate*

SHERWOOD ◉

Who only wants to sleep here? The well-being hotel with 14 rooms and apartments above Lake Wakatipu has much more to offer: yoga, meditation, Ayurvedan massage, live concerts, film nights, cocktail evenings and an excellent restaurant. *554 Frankton Road | tel. 03 4 50 10 90 | sherwoodqueenstown.nz | Moderate*

INFORMATION

DOC VISITOR CENTRE

50 Stanley Street | tel. 03 4 42 79 35 | www.doc.govt.nz

QUEENSTOWN I-SITE

Camp Street/Shotover Street | tel. 03 4 42 41 00 | www.queenstownisite.co.nz

WHERE TO GO

ARROWTOWN (158 C3) (ᗰ C15)

You only need to imagine the town without the souvenir shops, then Arrowtown 21 km/13.1 mi north of Queenstown resembles the gold-digger town that it once was. Old wooden houses and shops with saloon facades line Buckingham Street, and on Arrow River there are still the same huts owned by former Chinese gold prospectors in the forest. The river overgrown by trees, which is crossed by the black riders in "Lord of the Rings", has plenty of beautiful swimming spots. You can still pan for gold dust here in the water. You can also hire the pans on site. Just like during the gold rush, you can stay overnight in the *Historic Arrowtown Cottage (for 2 people | NZ$200/night | airbnb.com)* from 1890.

GLENORCHY (158 C3) (*𝄞 B–C15*)

The area around Glenorchy could be called Middle Earth because of the numerous Lord of the Rings film locations. In 45 minutes the *Road to paradise* from Queenstown leads to the small town at the north end of Lake Wakatipu. On the edge of Mount Aspiring National Park, where the film locations are situated like Lothlorien, Isengard and Amon Hen, the landscape is like a beautiful paradise – and it's very secluded. You can go horse-riding in the *Dart Valley (1hr riding tour for beginners NZ$140 | tel. 0800 32 78 53 | www.dartriver.co.nz)* or spend several hours exploring the long tributary of the Dart River on *Funyaks* (inflatable canoes) *(NZ$369 incl. lunch and jeep tour to locations from "Lord of the Rings" and "The Hobbit" | same provider).* Magical nature requires accommodation which quietly merges into the landscape. The blocks of cabins made from recycled wood are inconspicuous at 🌿 *The Headwaters (61 beds in dormitories and cabins | 34 Oban Street | tel. 03 4 09 04 01 | www.theheadwaters.co.nz | Expensive)* At the foot of the Richardson mountains, rainwater flows from the taps and electricity is generated with solar cells. The same operator also runs the nearby *Mrs Wolly's Campground* with three glamping tents *(Moderate)*. More information: www.glenorchyinfocentre.co.nz

MOUNT ASPIRING NATIONAL PARK (158–159 C–D 1–2) (*𝄞 B–C14*)

Mount Aspiring is New Zealand's Matterhorn. It towers 3,000 m/9,843 ft skywards and New Zealand's second largest national park is named after it. The park extends from Haast Pass to Lake Wakatipu and has impressive expansive valleys, glaciers, waterfalls and crystal-clear rivers. Famous hiking trails are the *Routeburn Track (in summer, book lodging in advance on www.doc.govt. nz | starting point car park at Routeburn Shelter, 68 km/42.3 mi north of Queens-*

In Mount Aspiring National Park hiking dreams come true

town) and *Caples Track (buy the Backcountry Hut Pass in advance in a Doc Office | starting point car park at the end of Greenstone Road, 86 km/53.4 mi north of Queenstown).* Tip: it's less busy on the tracks from Makaroa (130 km/81 mi north of Queenstown). For example, on the *Gillespies Pass* or *Wilkin Valley* with ascent to *Top Forks Hut*. On the half-day *Rob Roy Glacier Track (starting point at Raspberry Creek Carpark, 54 km/34 mi*

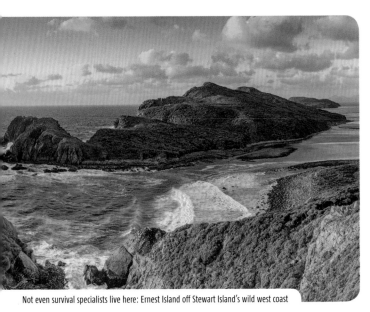

Not even survival specialists live here: Ernest Island off Stewart Island's wild west coast

west of Wanaka, 120 km/75 mi north of Queenstown on Wanaka–Mt Aspiring Road), you hike through the valley by Matukituki River, past waterfalls and to the glacier below Mount Rob Roy. At the viewpoint, keas (parrots) wait for your lunch. If you want to see as much as possible in a short time (and don't want to hike for very long), book the *Siberia Experience (NZ$395 | tel. 03 443 43 85 | siberiaexperience.co.nz)*, a 4 hr flight-hiking-jet boat tour which begins in Makaroa.

WANAKA (159 D2) (*C14–15*)

When travelling, you often think: we must do this and that. On Lake Wanaka, 70 km/43.5 mi north, you feel calm because nature takes over here. It's just as picturesque as in Queenstown, but no jet boats speed across the glacier lake, and paragliders are not constantly floating from the mountains (only occasionally). On shady pebble beaches you can spend the day dosing and enjoying a refreshing swim in the clear water. *Bremner Bay, Dublin Bay* and *Glendhu Bay* (hire a stand-up paddle board) are especially beautiful. Or you can visit the island of INSIDER TIP *Mou Waho* and go swimming in a lake which glistens light green and deserves the name of Paradise Lake. Tours are offered by Eco Wanaka Adventure *(4 hr | NZ$245 | tel. 0800 92 63 26 | www.ecowanaka.co.nz)*. A popular hiking route takes about 45 minutes to Mount Iron 250 m/820 ft above Wanaka. The ascent to Mount Roy (1,500 m/4,921 ft) is more exhausting. You complete the ascent and descent in about 7–8 hours, but your reward is a magnificent view of Mount Aspiring. The *food trucks* in the centre of Wanaka (51 Brownston Street) offer plenty of appetizing food, like *Burrito Craft (dai-*

ly noon–9pm | www.burritocraft.co.nz | *Budget*) or Francesca's Pizzas (daily 4pm–9pm | www.francescaspizzas.com | *Budget*). A few steps away is the *Cinema Paradiso (72 Brownston Street | www.paradiso.net.nz)*, the cinema theatre is filled with sofas. The restaurant ⊕ Ode (daily 6pm–11pm | 33 Ardmore Street | tel. 03 4 43 63 94 | www.odewanaka.com | *Expensive*) is a declaration of love to Wanaka. Here, almost 70 per cent of the food, which is served, is grown within a radius of 100 km/62 mi. There are only multi-course menus. The tour operator *Funny French Cars (from NZ$189 | funnyfrenchcars.co.nz)* drives you to the best vineyards in the area in old Citroens. The *Blue Pools*, 1.5 hours by car north of Wanaka, are incredibly beautiful. From the road, it's a 30-minute walk to the bathing pools with bright blue water in a rocky gorge in the rainforest. The skiing areas *Treble Cone* and *Cardrona* are open from June/July to early September, depending on the weather. Information: *Wanaka i-Site (103 Ardmore Street | tel. 03 4 43 12 33 | www.lakewanaka.co.nz)*

STEWART ISLAND

(158 B–C6) (*⌘ B17–18*) **If you want to make the trip to Rakiura, the "island of the glowing sky", as ★ Stewart Island is known by the Maoris, you must be keen: the journey over the choppy, 32 km/19.9 mi wide Foveaux Strait, the unpredictable weather and total seclusion don't tempt everyone.**

The island is almost as big as Tenerife, but only about 400 people live there – all in the unique location of *Oban*. The rest is unspoilt wilderness that still looks the same as thousands of years ago. The dense rainforest of Rakiura National Park is the habitat for 20,000 kiwis because here they hardly have any predators like cats, rats and possums. The emerald green sea sparkles invitingly in the summer sunshine, but it's ice cold. There are only 20 km/12.4 mi of roads, but 200 km/124 mi of hiking trails through unspoilt nature. Penguins waddle repeatedly over the road, and elsewhere on the island things are

BLOOD-THIRSTY MONSTERS

They say that New Zealand has no dangerous animals. That's true in comparison with Australia. The infamous sandfly falls into the category of vicious and nuisance animals: it's a small blackfly that mainly drives tourists crazy on South Island. It's not surprising; the beasts are guaranteed to find unprotected skin and their bites itch like mad for days. Sandflies find dark clothing totally irresistible.

The so-called pool hoovers drink a kind of blood broth and thrive on it. So, don't save on the insect repellent! DEET spray works well, but sprays with citronella or tea tree oil are supposed to repel sandflies. What should you do if there is a mass attack? Quickly run from the field, wave wildly with your arms and ideally dive under water. The question is who can hold their breath for longer …

different to other locations. Children learn at school to spend the night on their own in the rainforest, and the island's only policeman must repeatedly warn his fellow citizens not just to borrow someone else's cars – on the island, it's common to leave the key in the ignition. If you're lucky, on Stewart Island you can even see the ● *Aurora Australis (forecasts: aurora-service.net)*, the southern lights. Even in summer.

SIGHTSEEING

INSIDER TIP ▶ MASON BAY

In the wide bay, you will certainly not meet people but instead the most ● kiwis in the whole of New Zealand. You land on the wide sandy beach in a light propeller aircraft and are collected from here again in the evening. And between us: this unique experience is even better than the kiwi spotting tour. *From Oban | NZ$175 | 40 Elgin Terrace | tel. 03 218 9129 | www.stewartisland flights.com*

RAKIURA MUSEUM

Sperm whale teeth and portraits of emaciated emigrants: here, you get an impression of how hard life must have been for the early settlers and whalers on Stewart Island. *Mon–Sat 10am–1.30pm, Sun noon–2pm | NZ$2 | 9 Ayr Street | Oban | www.stewartisland.co.nz*

INSIDER TIP ▶ ULVA ISLAND

This must have been how New Zealand sounded when James Cook dropped anchor for the first time. On the uninhabited island, birds that are otherwise extinct tune up for proper concerts. "Bird whisperer" Ulva, a descendant of the first Maoris on Stewart Island, helps with the search for rare kaka parrots and flightless wekas. Kiwis occasionally even turn up

here during the daytime. Half-day tour incl. water taxi *(NZ$130 | tel. 03 219 12 16 | www.ulva.co.nz)* from Golden Bay Wharf (15-minutes' walk from the ferry wharf in Oban).

LEISURE & SPORTS

RAKIURA TRACK

On Stewart Island, there are only 20 km/12.4 mi of roads. You must explore the rest of the island on foot. For instance, on the 36 km/22.4 mi long Rakiura Track, which in three days takes you from Lee Bay to Fern Gully. You hike through dense rainforest across walkways and along secluded beaches. At night-time, you sleep in huts with wood ovens *(booking.doc.govt.nz)* and hear kiwis rustling in the bush. The tour starts in Lee Bay 7 km/4.4 mi north of Oban.

BIRDWATCHING

You're not so keen on birdwatching? Be inspired by *Angela Steffens'* enthusiasm for birds. On the *Ackers-at-dusk-Tour*, you can follow penguins with her at sunset and watch the sooty shearwaters that fly back to land in the evening and cry like babies in their caves on the forest floor. *Nov–March | NZ$100 | tel. 027 3 16 30 77 | www.beaksandfeath ers.co.nz*

WILD KIWI ENCOUNTER

When kiwis use their long beaks at night to hunt for fleas in the sand, you have a very good chance of spotting one of these timid animals. *Real Journeys* takes you by boat at sunset to one of the island's remote parts, where you join guides to go looking for kiwis. Please remember: seals sleep in the dunes and don't want to be disturbed! *Duration: approx. 4 hr | NZ$199 | www.real journeys.co.nz*

ENTERTAINMENT

SOUTH SEA HOTEL

Photos of crashed aircraft and whales cut open are on the walls, men with bronzed faces at the bar: it's party time at the bottom of the world! In the island's only pub, tourists and island residents dance spontaneously among the tables or sit at the piano. The highlight every Sunday is the pub quiz, where in 2015 Prinz Harry even participated during his trip of the Commonwealth. Deep-fried green lipped mussels taste good with the beer. *26 Elgin Terrace | Oban | tel. 03 2191059 | www.stewart-island.co.nz | Moderate*

WHERE TO STAY

OBSERVATION ROCK LODGE ☼

The boutique hotel is hidden away on a hill in the rainforest. At breakfast, kaka parrots fly in through the kitchen window and in the evening the owner Annett prepares multi-course menus for you with island ingredients. A dream view of the sea and bright red sunsets. *4 rooms | 7 Leonard Street | Oban | tel. 03 2191444 | www.observationrocklodge.co.nz | Expensive*

STEWART ISLAND BACKPACKERS

Bearded travellers, penguin fans and rucksack tourists: in the simple, clean hostel, the guests share four-bed rooms and adventure stories with each other. There are also double rooms and a camp ground. You can hire the tents and mats. *76 places | 18 Ayr Street | Oban | tel. 03 2191114 | www.stewartislandbackpackers.co.nz | Budget*

ARRIVAL

From Bluff, you can travel for 1 hr in the catamaran *Foveaux Express (depending on season up to 4 times daily | NZ$85 one way | tel. 03 2127660 | www.stewartislandexperience.co.nz)* over the waves and oyster beds to Stewart Island. The strait is

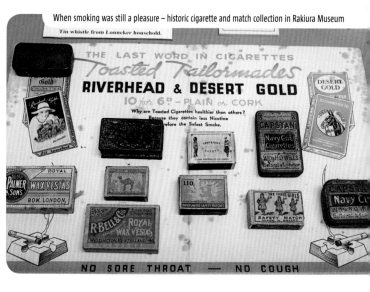

When smoking was still a pleasure – historic cigarette and match collection in Rakiura Museum

famous for its stormy weather. It's a good idea to bring some seasickness tablets! From Invercargill, you can fly to Stewart Island *(3 times daily | NZ$215 return trip | tel. 03 218 91 29 | www.stewartisland flights.com)*.

INFORMATION

RAKIURA NATIONAL PARK VISITOR CENTRE
15 Main Road | Oban | tel. 03 219 00 09 | www.doc.govt.nz

OBAN VISITOR INFORMATION
12 Elgin Terrace | tel. 03 219 00 56 | www.stewartisland.co.nz

WHERE TO GO

BLUFF (158 C5) (*C17*)
A small coastal town with weather-beaten wooden houses. The only luxury in the area are the bountiful oysters in the sea

(March–Aug.). With a photo from *Stirling Point* you can prove to your friends that you made it to the bottom of the world. A sign says that from here it's only another 4,810 km/2,989 mi to the South Pole. Appropriately, nearby is a hotel called ✵ *Land's End (5 rooms | 10 Warde Parade | tel. 03 212 75 75 | www.landsend hotel.co.nz | Expensive)* – a whitewashed building with modern Brit chic furniture and a magnificent ocean vista.

INVERCARGILL (158 C5) (*C17*)
Just before you fall into the sea at New Zealand's southernmost point, there is another town that only a handful of visitors pay attention to. Invercargill, with its chequerboard layout and population of 55,000, at first looks rather dreary. But if you look more closely, you discover magnificent Victorian buildings in the whole of the town, for example, the 1889 *Water Tower* or *Civic Theatre* from 1906. The residents are proud of their museum

Not digital wallpaper: Milford Sound can really look like this – if the weather is fine!

Transport World (daily 10am–5pm | NZ$25 | 491 Tay Street | www.transport world.co.nz) with one of the world's biggest old-timer collections. The Fat Bastard Pies (Mon–Fri 6am–4pm | 158 Tay Street | Budget) are considered the best in the country. In Safari Lodge (4 rooms | 51 Herbert Street | tel. 0800 88 55 57 | www.safarilodge.co.nz | Expensive) in a historic villa you spend the night in antique four-poster beds. Information: Invercargill i-Site (112 Gala Street | tel. 03 211 08 95 | southlandnz.com, www.inver cargillnz.com)

RIVERTON (158 B–C5) (*M* B17)

A small artists' eco community with fishing harbour and light wooden houses. Locals rent out holiday houses (booka bach.co.nz) on the long sandy beach. In the Te Hikoi Museum (Oct–March daily 10am–5pm, April–Sept 10am–4pm | NZ$8 | 172 Palmerston Street | www.tehikoi.co.nz) everything is about the close relationship between Maoris and European settlers at New Zealand's southern tip. Reconstructions of old huts and whaling boats make the past come alive. On Gemstone Beach 30 km/18.6 mi further north you find semi-precious stones like quartz and jade on the beach.

TE ANAU

(158 B3) (*M* B15) **The small Te Anau on Lake Te Anau is the starting point for tours through New Zealand's biggest national park Fiordland.**

Behind South Island's biggest lake you can already see the summits of the Unesco World Natural Heritage site soaring upwards. In the cafés you can listen to the hikers' expedition tales. Large swathes of the national park, which is about half the size of Sicily, are still unexplored and belong only to the Fiordland penguins, dolphins, kea parrots and sandflies. Humans are only guests in this wilderness world – at Milford and Doubtful Sound or on the three Great Walks Milford, Routeburn and Kepler.

SIGHTSEEING

GLOWWORM CAVES

By boat, it takes 30 minutes from Te Anau to reach a glowworm cave. This is a fascinating underworld where the green glow of the mosquito larvae provide light and the waterfalls cascade in the darkness. In small boats, you explore with Real Journeys (duration 2.5 hr incl. transport | from NZ$93 | tel. 0800 65 65 01 | www.realjourneys.co.nz) the meandering river system inside the caves.

LEISURE & SPORTS

HIKING TOURS

Do you want to explore nature alone, or with a guide? For just a few hours, or several days? Three Great Walks are possible from Te Anau. The most well-known is the ☆ Milford Track, which the first settlers already built in 1880, to travel from Lake Te Anau to Milford Sound. The popular tour takes 4 days with stopovers in huts. You should definitely book several months in advance at Fiordland National Park Visitor Centre (hut NZ$140/night | no camping! | tel. 03 249 79 24 | www.greatwalks. co.nz)! The same applies for the ☆ Kepler Track (hut NZ$130, tent pitch NZ$40/night), a 60 km/37.3 mi long circuit, which takes 3–4 days through valleys formed by glaciers and mountains with views of Lake Te Anau. The track begins and ends at Kepler Carpark 5 km/3.1 mi from Te Anau and is suitable for day trips (e.g. along Waiau River to Rainbow Reach). In the direction of Mount Aspiring National Park, the ✹ Routeburn Track (huts NZ$130, tent pitch NZ$40/night) heads towards Mount Aspiring National Park through an Alpine wonderland with waterfalls and majestic summits. You need 2–4 days for the 33 km/20.5 mi from The Divide Shelter on Milford Road (85 km/52.8 mi from Te Anau) to the Routeburn Shelter near Glenorchy. *Trips & Tramps (tel. 03 2 49 70 81 | tripsandtramps.com)* and *Fiordland Outdoors (tel. 021 1 97 45 55 | www.fiordlandoutdoors.co.nz)* organize guided day trips along the Great Walks.

WHERE TO STAY

BLUE THISTLE COTTAGES ✹
Spacious cottages 2.5 km/1.6 mi from Te Anau on a hill with a lake view and each with a kitchen and private garden. *4 cottages | 168 Te Anau-Milford Highway | tel. 03 2 49 83 38 | bluethistlecottages.com | Expensive*

TE ANAU LAKEVIEW KIWI HOLIDAY PARK & MOTELS
How much money is left in the holiday kitty? Here, there is accommodation for every budget: in huts, motel rooms, a backpacker hostel or on camping grounds for campers by the lake. *77 Manapouri-Te Anau Highway | tel. 03 2 49 74 57 | teanauholidaypark.co.nz | Budget–Moderate*

INFORMATION

FIORDLAND NATIONAL PARK VISITOR CENTRE
Lakefront Drive | Te Anau | tel. 03 2 49 79 24 | www.greatwalks.co.nz, www.fiordland.org.nz

WHERE TO GO

DOUBTFUL SOUND ✹
(158 A3) (⁄⁄ A15)
Three times longer, with more channels and less touristy than Milford Sound – and more difficult to reach. As no road goes to the 40 km/24.9 mi long fjord, you have to depend on transport with tour operators. They will take you by boat across Lake Manapouri and then by bus over Wilmot Pass to the ferry wharf at Doubtful Sound *(journey time approx. 2 hr)*. On the fjord you are unlikely to meet another boat, and the famous *Sound of Silence* in this area is better to listen to than on Milford Sound. The countryside is so beautiful that it is tempting to look at it through the camera viewfinder. But then you're guaranteed to miss the moment when the dolphin jumps out of the water. You can occasionally pack away your equipment and enjoy what photos cannot capture: the fragrance of the dense green, the humid air and the graceful mountain giants. A day trip incl. cruise in the sound costs about *NZ$250* or INSIDER TIP 2-day tour incl. transport and 5-hour kayak tour per day as well as overnight stay in tents about NZ$430 – both with *Go Orange (tel. 03 4 42 73 40 | www.goorange.co.nz)*. Although it's expensive, a real experience are the overnight cruises incl. transport, dinner, a night on board and kayak excursions for about NZ$500–700 with *Real Journeys (tel. 03 2 49 60 00 | www.realjourneys.co.nz)*. Tip: before you depart, stay overnight in the historic ✹ *Murrell's Grand View House (4 rooms | Murrell Avenue | Manapouri | tel. 03 2 49 66 42 | murrells.co.nz | Expensive)*, which is 20 minutes by car from Te Anau. This is a B & B in a historic wooden villa with a priceless view of Lake Manapouri.

Tricky to reach: the seabirds on Doubtful Sound still outnumber the tourists

MILFORD SOUND ★ ⁂
(158 B2) (*B14*)

Milford Sound in fine or bad weather is like the difference between colour and black-and-white photography: in the sunshine, the moss-covered cliff faces of the 15 km/9.3 mi long fjord shine a luminous green colour, the rainbows glisten in the numerous waterfalls, and when dolphins jump out of the bright blue water, nature looks as kitschy and beautiful as a spray-paint mural. If it rains, suddenly the landscape only consists of grey tones. The mountain peaks disappear into the clouds and the water looks black – and this has its own special drama. With 200 rainy days and up to 8 m/26.2 ft of rain per annum the chances are high that you will arrive on a grey day. But you shouldn't miss the chance to take a boat trip into the mountains. The 1,692 m/5,551 ft high *Mitre Peak* on the fjord soars like a cathedral into the sky and the passengers on the excursion boats gasp "amazing" and "breathtaking". Arriving via *Milford Road* (120 km/75 mi from Te Anau) in a mountain setting filled with waterfalls, lakes and rivers is also an amazing spectacle. However, be prepared to share Milford Sound with plenty of other people. You can choose e. g.: a 2-hour tour to Tasman Sea *(NZ$85 | tel. 03 2 49 81 10 | www.mitrepeak.com)*, a 4-hour boat excursion incl. 1hr kayak tour *(NZ$179 | tel. 0800 26 45 36 | southerndiscoveries.co.nz)*, a kayak tour at sunrise to the highest waterfall, *Lady Bowens Falls (2 hr | NZ$109 | tel. 0800 47 67 26 | www. roscosmilfordkayaks.com)*. You can enjoy real silence on paddle tours incl. a short hike along the Milford Track *(1 hr kayak tour and 3.5 hr hike | NZ$129 | tel. 0800 47 67 26 | www.roscosmilfordkayaks. com)*. The only option to stop overnight in the area is *Milford Sound Lodge (www. milfordlodge.com)* with different priced rooms and attractive chalets. Don't forget to fill the car with petrol before departing in Te Anau!

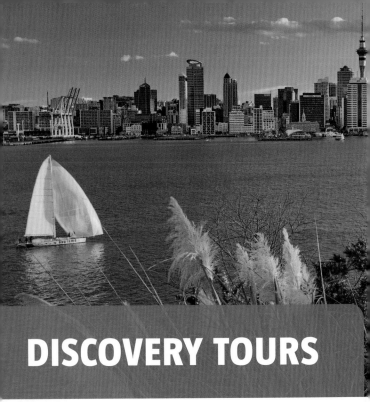

DISCOVERY TOURS

① NEW ZEALAND AT A GLANCE

START: ① Auckland **END:** ㉚ Christchurch	24 days Driving time (without stops) 54 hours
Distance: ➡ 3,600 km/2,237 mi	

COSTS: approx. NZ$10,000 for two people (incl. petrol, rental car, car ferry, food & drink, excursions, accommodation)

IMPORTANT TIPS: New Zealand has few motorways, most roads are single track and two-way travel, often narrow and with lots of bends; travel times are often longer than planned. Depending on the weather, you can fly from ㉖ Queenstown to the famous Milford Sound → p. 113. The Scenic Flight *(from NZ$395 | milfordflights.co.nz)* takes one hour.

Would you like to explore the places that are unique to this country? Then the Discovery Tours are just the thing for you – they include terrific tips for stops worth making, breathtaking places to visit, selected restaurants and fun activities. It's even easier with the Touring App: download the tour with map and route to your smartphone using the QR Code on pages 2/3 or from the website address in the footer below – and you'll never get lost again even when you're offline.

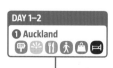

TOURING APP

→ p. 2/3

Fjords, glaciers, secluded beaches, mountains, rainforests and warm rivers – in New Zealand, the scenery changes almost after every street corner. But which places are well worth a visit? On this tour, despite the short time, you will see as much as possible of Aotearoa – and can enjoy the experience with no stress.

You're ready to set off in ❶ Auckland → p. 33. Walk along the waterfront to the restaurants and cafés at Viaduct Harbour and in the evening from Sky Tower survey the sea of lights in the city. In the morning, you enjoy breakfast at Café Dizengoff (daily 6.30am–4pm | 256 Ponsonby

DAY 1–2

❶ Auckland

🍽 ☀ 🍴 🚶 🎒 🛏

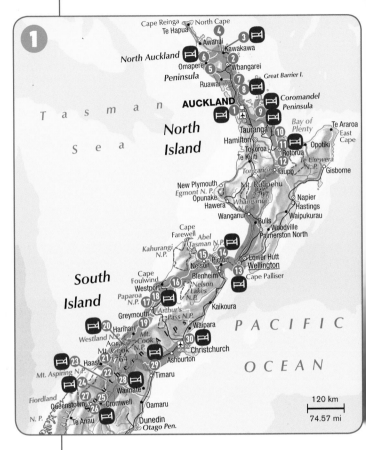

1

Cape Reinga — North Cape
Te Hapua
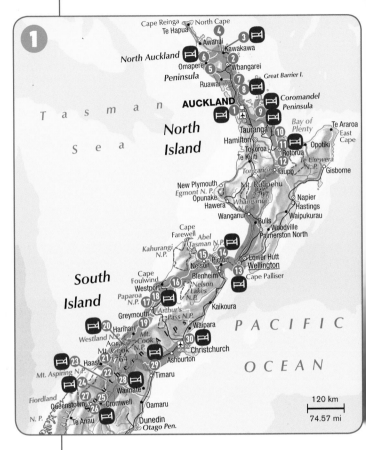 3
Awanui
North Auckland 6 Kawakawa
Omapere 5 Whangarei
Peninsula
Ruawai 7 Great Barrier I.
8
AUCKLAND Coromandel
1 9 Peninsula
Bay of Te Araroa
Tauranga Plenty East
Hamilton 10 Cape
Tokoroa 11 Opotiki
Te Kuiti Rotorua
12 Te Urewera Gisborne
Tongariro N.P.
New Plymouth Taupo
Egmont N.P. Mt. Ruapehu
Opunake 2797
Hawera Napier
Whanganui Hastings
Wanganui Waipukurau
Bulls
Woodville
Cape Palmerston North
Farewell Abel
Kahurangi Tasman N.P.
N.P. 15 14 Lower Hutt
Nelson Picton Wellington
Cape Blenheim 13
Foulwind Nelson Cape Palliser
Westport Lakes
Paparoa 16 N.P.
N.P. 17 18 Kaikoura
Greymouth Arthur's
19 Pass N.P.
20 Harihari Waipara
Westland N.P. Mt. 30
Aoraki/ 21 Cook Christchurch
23 Mt. Cook 29 Ashburton
Haast 3764
22 28 Timaru
Mt. Aspiring N.P. 24
27 25 Waimate
Queenstown Cromwell Oamaru
Te Anau 26
Fiordland Dunedin
N.P. Otago Pen.

Tasman Sea

North Island

South Island

PACIFIC

OCEAN

120 km
74.57 mi

Road | tel. 09 3 60 01 08 | Budget) in the trendy district
of Ponsonby and stroll around the area's second-hand
shops and boutiques. In the afternoon, there is still
time to view contemporary art in **Auckland Art Gallery**
*(daily 10am–5pm | NZ$20 | Wellesley Street E | auck-
landartgallery.com)* with its impressive atrium made of
Kauri wood.

DAY 3–4

201 km/125 mi

2 Matapouri Bay

87 km/54.1 mi

Head for the sea! **In the north, past Auckland** the traffic gets lighter and the dream beaches of **Tutukaka Coast**
come into view. Stop for a swim on the golden beach at
2 Matapouri Bay and continue to the **Bay of Islands**. In
early evening check in here in the small coastal town of

❸ **Russell →** p. 41 for two nights at the **Duke of Marlborough** – a white wooden villa with colonial charm and a sea view. Next day, during a half-day **boat tour** *(NZ$117 | tel. 0800 65 33 39 | dolphincruises.co.nz)* explore the most beautiful bays in the Bay of Islands and go swimming with the dolphins.

The first stop of the day are the ❹ **Waitangi Treaty Grounds →** p. 42. Afterwards, drive to ❺ **Waipoua Kauri Forest →** p. 44 **on the west coast.** Here, **Tane Mahuta**, a kauri tree 51 m/167.3 ft tall, soars above the forest. The God of the forest is reputedly 2,000 years old. Stop overnight at ❻ **Oponomi Hotel** *(9 rooms | 19 SH 12 | tel. 09 4 05 88 58 | opononihotel.com | Moderate)* in Omapere at Hokianga Harbour with a view of the gigantic dunes of Rangi Point. In the morning, **head back southwards** to the **Hauraki Gulf**, where you spend the rest of the day on the beautiful ❼ INSIDERTIP **Pakiri Beach**. In the evening, head for the ❽ INSIDERTIP **Sawmill Café** *(9 rooms/ apartments | 142 Pakiri Road | tel. 09 4 22 60 19 | sawmill cafe.co.nz | Budget)* in the nearby surfer town Leigh. After you've enjoyed a quiet dinner (e.g. fresh snapper or ceviche), local bands take over the stage later in the evening. Then, simply fall into bed here – the restaurant also offers rooms.

Carry on to the ❾ **Coromandel Peninsula →** p. 45. First, stop in the old gold rush location of **Coromandel Town** at the **Oyster Company** *(daily 10am–5pm | 1611 Manaia Road | freshoysters.co.nz | Budget)*, a wooden shack by the sea, where you can get fresh oysters. The beach at **Hahei** is a really beautiful beach with its fine sand and turquoise-blue sea, where you can stay at **Tatahi Lodge** *(6 rooms | 9 Grange Road | tel. 07 8 66 39 92 | tatahilodge.co.nz | Moderate)* with a sub-tropical garden. In the morning, set off on a kayak tour from the beach *(3 hr | NZ$115 | kayaktours.co.nz)* to the cliff caves of **Cathedral Cove** and then dig on **Hot Water Beach** with tourists from around the world for the hot springs (bring a spade!). If you don't like crowded beaches, carry on to the wild bay of INSIDERTIP **Opoutere Beach** and enjoy a wonderful picnic hidden away in the dunes behind a pine forest. Stay the night at the popular surfer spot **Whangamata**, where seagulls in the numerous cafés along Port Road steal pommes frites off your plate. At the hotel INSIDERTIP **Surf N Stay** *(6 rooms | 227 Beverley*

❸ Russell

DAY 5–6

74 km/46 mi

❹ Waitangi Treaty Grounds

120 km/75 mi

❺ Waipoua Kauri Forest

35 km/21.8 mi

❻ Oponomi Hotel

210 km/130 mi

❼ Pakiri Beach

12 km/7.5 mi

❽ Sawmill Café

DAY 7–8

208 km/129 mi

❾ Coromandel Peninsula

Terrace | tel. 07 8 65 83 23 | surfnstaynewzealand.com | Budget) near the wide beach full of spray, you can book a board and surfing course along with your room.

DAY 9–10

273 km / 170 mi

⑩ **Mount Maunganui**

75 km / 46.6 mi

⑪ **Rotorua**

28 km / 17.4 mi

⑫ **Kerosene Creek**

468 km / 291 mi

⑬ **Wellington**

119 km / 74 mi

⑭ **The Portage Hotel**

First thing in the morning, head for ⑩ **Mount Maunganui** → p. 58 and climb the mountain with a panoramic view of the ocean (approx. 45 min). Then, enjoy a refreshing swim in the sea and lunch on the waterfront. In the late afternoon you arrive at the steaming thermal region of ⑪ **Rotorua** → p. 53. In the Maori village **Te Puia** you can dine in the evening at the **Te Po Experience** *(daily 6.15pm | NZ$125 | Hemo Road | tel. 07 3 48 90 47 | tepuia.com)* and enjoy a festive meal of Hangi (made in a ground oven) and watch a Haka warrior dance. Next day, avoid the expensive thermal baths and drive to ⑫ **Kerosene Creek 30 km/18.6 mi south** – this river has warm water and is in the middle of the forest! Now, get ready for the tour's longest stretch in the car. However, it's definitely not boring because **the route to Wellington** mainly passes through wonderful fantasy film landscapes. **Along Desert Road and past Tongariro National Park** with snow-covered volcanic summits and **on the SH1 along the beautiful Kapiti Coast**. In the evening, you arrive in ⑬ **Wellington** → p. 63.

DAY 11–12

Baristas are the new DJs – at least in New Zealand's coffee capital. Start the day with a flat white or cold brew in one of the more than 300 cafés like e.g. **Flight Coffee Hangar** *(Mon–Fri 7am–4pm, Sat/Sun 8am–5pm | 119 Dixon Street | flightcoffee.co.nz)*. In the **cable car** you travel to the **Botanic Gardens above the city** with a spectacular panoramic view over Wellington and stroll back to the centre. From **Cuba Street**, New Zealand's reputedly coolest street, with its numerous art galleries, shops and graffiti walls it's only a few steps to the interactive **Te Papa Tongarewa** by the sea where every item on display defines New Zealand's heritage, including Maori canoes, simulated earthquakes and Moa bones. **In the late afternoon, catch the ferry to South Island** and enjoy the view of the **Marlborough Sounds** when the sunset bathes the coastal scenery in deep orange. From the ferry wharf in **Picton** → p. 98 carry on by boat to the ⑭ **The Portage Hotel** *(41 rooms | 2923 Kenepuru Road | tel. 03 5 73 43 09 | portage.co.nz | Moderate)* which is situated in a beautiful dense green location on Kenepuru Sound. Wake up with a view of the light blue sparkling sea and spend a day exploring in kayaks.

Pause in Picton – preferably with a view over the water and ferries to North Island

In the morning, **the boat takes you to Picton**. You can get in your hire car again and explore ⑮ **Nelson** → **p. 94**, before heading for **the sparsely populated west coast**. Wind your way through ⑯ **Buller Gorge**, where you can walk across New Zealand's longest swing bridge. In the early afternoon, you arrive at **Punakaiki** → **p. 91**. The main attraction here are the ⑰ **Pancake Rocks** where the wild Tasman Bay bubbles up. In the rainforest behind the beach in Te Miko are the wonderful wooden cottages of the ⑱ **Te Nikau Retreat** *(10 cottages | 19 Hartmount Place | tel. 03 7 311111 | tenikauretreat.co.nz | Budget)*. On one of the most spectacular coast roads in the world, next day you **head further south**. If you are travelling with children, on the way in the Shantytown → p. 137 near Greymouth you notice a little of the gold-digger atmosphere. The others can continue to ⑲ **Hokitika** → **p. 92**. Here, it's all about the *Greenstone* because the rivers near the town are rich in jade. At **Bonz 'n' Stonz** you can even design and polish a lucky charm. In the early evening, finally the ⑳ **Franz Josef Glacier** → **p. 87** comes into view with its massive ice flows. Overnight, sleep surrounded by the dense rainforest at the ⓦ **Te Waonui Forest Retreat** *(24 rooms | 3 Wallace Street |*

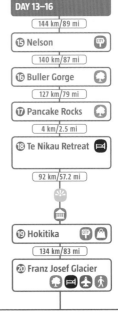

DAY 13–16

144 km / 89 mi

⑮ Nelson

140 km / 87 mi

⑯ Buller Gorge

127 km / 79 mi

⑰ Pancake Rocks

4 km / 2.5 mi

⑱ Te Nikau Retreat

92 km / 57.2 mi

⑲ Hokitika

134 km / 83 mi

⑳ Franz Josef Glacier

94 km/58.4 mi

㉑ Lake Paringa 🌿 🌳

121 km/75 mi

㉒ Blue Pools 💦

9 km/5.6 mi

㉓ Mountain View Lodge 🛏

DAY 17–18

㉔ Wanaka 🌿 🚶 🎿 🚴 🛏

DAY 19–20

31 km/19.3 mi

㉕ Cardrona Hotel 🍴

40 km/24.9 mi

㉖ Queenstown 💦 🎿 🚴 🍸 🍴 🛏

50 km/31.1 mi

㉗ Glenorchy 🎬 🌳

DAY 21–22

246 km/153 mi

㉘ Lake Ohau 🌳 🛏

179 km/111 mi

tel. 03 357 19 19 | tewaonui.co.nz | Expensive) with a view of snow-covered mountains. Early next morning your **Heli-Hike** *(NZ$449 | helicopter.co.nz)* begins to the glacier, where you clamber through the unique ice landscape for two hours with a mountain guide. Before continuing next day **to the Haast Pass inland,** you should definitely stop to take photos at the crystal-clear **㉑ Lake Paringa**. Here, the mountains and forests are reflected in the water! In the early evening you arrive at the **㉒ Blue Pools** in a rock gorge with bright blue glacier water. Jump into the ice-cold water and then fall into a deep sleep in the nearby **㉓** INSIDER TIP **Mountain View Lodge** *(5 rooms | 53 Rata Road | tel. 03 443 15 32 | makarora.com | Moderate)* in Makarora in the heart of **Mount Aspiring National Park → p. 105.**

These mountains separate worlds. If the stormy weather on the west coast made it necessary to wear a fleece, in the morning in **㉔ Wanaka → p. 106** in Central Otago it is probably warm and sunny. Relax for a couple of days in the many bays of **Lake Wanaka** with a view of **Mount Aspiring**. If you're hiking, enjoy the Pinot Noir at **Rippon Vineyard** and the magnificent countryside and stretch your legs on a bike tour along the lake. In the morning, **continue on a winding pass road south** towards hectic Queenstown. On the way, you can enjoy a pleasant meal in the restaurant of the old **㉕ Cardrona Hotel** *(daily 9am–10pm | 2312 Cardrona Valley Road | tel. 03 443 8153 | cardronahotel.co.nz | Moderate)* with gold rush flair. The venison fillet is a hit! In **㉖ Queenstown → p. 100** you will be amazed how touristy New Zealand can be. Get your adrenalin shot from river rafting, bungy jumping or paragliding – or take in the magnificent mountain panorama during a peaceful hike or bike tour. When Queenstown fades in the dimmed night lighting, it's time for a pub tour. Excellent live bands play e.g. at the ♥ **Sherwood Hotel** *(554 Frankton Road | sherwood queenstown.nz | Moderate)* with cocktail bar, where you can also enjoy healthy and nutritious meals. You should plan a half day for **㉗ Glenorchy → p. 105.** Here, the boundaries are blurred between cinema and reality because so many "Lord of the Rings" scenes were filmed around town.

In the morning, if you turn **off the SH8 to Lake Ohau** you will almost be the only car on the road, as most tourists carry onto Lake Pukaki or Lake Tekapo. **㉘ Lake Ohau** sparkles just as wonderfully blue – and you can enjoy it all to yourself. In the region's only accommodation at **Lake Ohau Lodge** *(72 rooms | tel. 03 4 38 98 85 | ohau. co.nz | Moderate)* above the lake at the most you will meet a few cyclists who are on the *Alps 2 Ocean Trail*. Despite the view of **Mount Cook**, the rooms are not overpriced. Do you like swimming in mountain rivers? Then, you will love ㉙ **Geraldine** in the heart of South Canterbury. Around the small town at the foot of the Alps there are plenty of good swimming spots in the middle of an impressive Wild West landscape like in **Te Moana** (with waterfall!). 20 minutes by car outside the town (pop. 3,500) you can stay overnight at the **Waikonini Homestead** *(7 rooms | Horsfall Road 300 | tel. 03 6 96 38 68 | waikoninihome stead.co.nz | Budget)*, a B&B in a historic wooden villa on the edge of Peel Forest.

In ㉚ **Christchurch → p. 76**, find out how the city is re-inventing itself with creative ideas after the earthquake in 2011. In what was the almost completely destroyed city centre in recent years the world's best **street art artists** *(Street Art Walking Tours with Watch This Space | NZ$30 | tel.021 113 85 02 | watchthisspace.org.nz)* have created giant wall murals. INSIDER TIP ▶ **Smash Palace** *(172 High Street | thesmashpalace.co.nz)* is a bar made from old buses and containers and there is a **Cardboard Cathedral** *(234 Hereford Street)*. In the early evening, **Cassels Brewery** *(3 Garlands Road | tel. 03 3 89 53 59 | casselsbrewery. co.nz | Budget)* is worth a visit for pizzas and craft beer – it's in **The Tannery**, a restored Victorian tannery full of boutiques and cafés in the district of Woolston. In the evening, you can check into your room at the **Eco Villa** *(8 rooms | 251 Hereford Street | tel. 03 5 95 13 64 | ecovil la.co.nz | Moderate)* with outdoor tubs in the garden. You can relax here in the dark in the warm water and take a last look at the Southern Cross.

Memorial in white: empty chairs opposite the cardboard cathedral in Christchurch

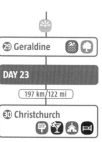

㉙ Geraldine

DAY 23

197 km / 122 mi

㉚ Christchurch

2

GREAT BARRIER ISLAND – DISCOVERY TOUR ON THE ECO ISLAND

START: ❶ Auckland END: ❶ Auckland	3 days Driving time (without stops) 10½ hours
Distance: 🚗 300 km/186 mi	

COSTS: approx. NZ$875/person (incl. ferry, hire car, petrol, accommodation and food, activities)

IMPORTANT TIP: Infrastructure is limited so you should organize everything for the tour and book ahead *(greatbarrier.co.nz)*.
From Christmas to mid-January, the number of residents doubles – it's a good time to avoid!

New Zealand as it was 40 years ago – no electricity grid, no main water supply or waste disposal. The 900 residents of ⭐ **The Barriers** are charmingly alternative, creative and nature is unspoilt: white beaches, picturesque bays, wonderful hikes, hot springs and lots of zones with no mobile reception.

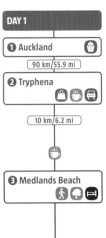

DAY 1

❶ Auckland

⟶ 90 km/55.9 mi

❷ Tryphena

⟶ 10 km/6.2 mi

❸ Medlands Beach

From the Sealink ferry terminal *(www.sealink.co.nz)* in the **Wynyard Quarter** in ❶ **Auckland** → p. 33 **the ferry takes you early morning on a 4.5 hr-tour past beautiful islands through the Hauraki Gulf to the ❷ Tryphena**, the main town on Great Barrier. Hire car companies come to the harbour. **Shoal Bay Pottery** *(Shoal Bay Road)* is the first port of call and is about 3 minutes from the terminal; it has beautiful handcrafted ceramics and beach art. Head to **Stonewall Village** for a snack – this is Tryphena's mini-centre with the largest of the three island shops and a few restaurants. **Pa Beach Café is pleasant**. Then, head for ❸ **Medlands Beach**. The sleepy town on the long beach is **10 minutes away on the eastern side of the island.** Sand, waves and a few holiday houses – an idyllic retreat. Check in for two nights at the **Medlands Beach Lodge** *(3 rooms | 149 Sandhills Road | tel. 09 4 29 03 35 | medlandsbeachlodge.com | Expensive)*, a pleasant B & B with beach views. The owner, Mark, is a perfect host for his guests; his home-baked bread tastes like back home. Vicky from the **Waiora Beach Retreat** *(53 Sandhills Road | tel. 09 4 29 01 29 | waiorabeachretreat.nz)* helps you during the three-hour **Nature Forest Therapy Walk** *(NZ$75)* to

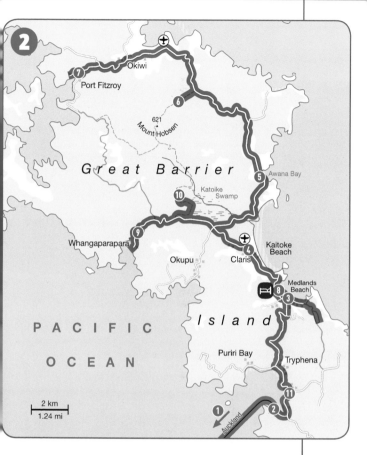

use all your senses and go barefoot to explore Medland's nature. In the evening, simply cook dinner in Mark's kitchen. After dark, count shooting stars with the star guides from **Good Heavens** (NZ$90 | Medlands Beach | tel. 09 4 29 08 76 | goodheavens.co.nz). Since 2017, the Barrier is one of three INSIDER TIP ▶ Dark Sky Sanctuaries worldwide; away from any light pollution you can hardly see the sky for the stars. That's thanks to the giant telescope and fantastic information.

Start the day with a swim, go surfing or enjoy a walk on Medlands Beach, **then head for the lonely north.** On the way in ❹ **Claris** you can stock up with supplies,

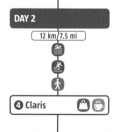

DAY 2

12 km / 7.5 mi

❹ Claris

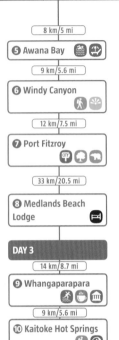

8 km/5 mi

⑤ Awana Bay

9 km/5.6 mi

⑥ Windy Canyon

12 km/7.5 mi

⑦ Port Fitzroy

33 km/20.5 mi

⑧ Medlands Beach Lodge

DAY 3

14 km/8.7 mi

⑨ Whangaparapara

9 km/5.6 mi

⑩ Kaitoke Hot Springs

19 km/11.8 mi

there is a shop here and the café **My Fat Puku** *(Facebook: myfatpuku)* for a good coffee break. **Turn right onto Gray Road, after 10 minutes you arrive at ⑤ Awana Bay**, another dream bay for swimming and relaxation. Then, carry on to the starting point of a 15-minute short walk to **⑥ Windy Canyon. Drive slowly, otherwise you will miss the sign on the left-hand side!** Steps lead into the gorge surrounded by steep rock faces swept by the wind. **Carry on until you see the spectacular view!** Then, continue driving as far as **⑦ Port Fitzroy**, a beautiful, protected natural harbour with the island's third shop. During the walk through **Glenfern Sanctuary** *(NZ$40 | Glenfern Road | tel. 09 4 29 00 91)*, a reserve with local plants and birds, a guided tour is worthwhile. You should book in advance! Take the same way back in the evening to the **⑧ Medlands Beach Lodge**.

On the last day in **⑨ Whangaparapara** explore the west coast on the SUP board, which you can hire from **Shiny Paua Stand** *(NZ$25/hr | tel. 09 4 29 06 03)*. Then, explore the **old whaling station** on the quay with information about New Zealand's inglorious whaling era. **Take the same road back. After 3.5 km/2.2 mi on the left is the start of the 45-minute bush hike to the ⑩ Kaitoke Hot Springs**, natural thermal springs in the middle of the bush. Take swimwear with you! **Then, drive back about 40 min-**

Enjoy a flat white in Napier with the Art Deco backdrop

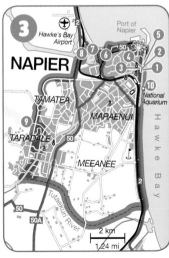

utes to ⑪ **Tryphena**; at 3pm the ferry departs for ❶ **Auckland**. Check-in is at 2pm and you arrive in the **Wynyard Quarter** about 7.30pm, perfect timing for dinner in the trendy harbour quarter.

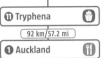

⑪ Tryphena

92 km/57.2 mi

❶ Auckland

③ ART DECO & WINE – BIKING TOUR AROUND NAPIER

START: ❶ Napier City Bike Hire END: ❶ Napier City Bike Hire	4–6 hours Driving time (without stops) 2¼ hours
Distance: 🚲 36 km/22 mi	

COSTS: About NZ$100/person incl. bike hire, lunch, admission

IMPORTANT TIP: Book your bike in advance from ❶ **Napier City Bike Hire** *(117 Marine Parade | tel. 0800 24 53 44 | bikehirenapier.co.nz)* opposite the i-Site mit flexiblen pick-up-/drop-off times.
Most of the route is signposted as the *Napier City Loop* with white routemarkers. Download the App *Napier Art Deco* beforehand with details of the architecture.
Reserve at table at the ❾ **Mission Estate** at tel. *06 8 45 93 54*!

You can expect great variety in Hawke's Bay – on one of the flat bike circuits around Napier with Art Deco buildings and expansive wetlands, with exquisite wines, green water meadows and never-ending coasts.

10:00am Collect your bike from ❶ **Napier City Bike Hire on Marine Parade opposite the i-Site.** To start with, take a quick tour of the city. The App *Napier Art Deco* informs you about the most important buildings. **Cross over the street and cycle in a southerly direction for a while, then turn right into Albion Street and right again into Hastings Street.** After about 200 m/650 ft you will see the ❷ **ASB Bank** and the first impressive historic building. Head inside and look upwards: a unique mixture of Maori symbols and Art Deco decorates the ceiling. **Then, turn left into Tennyson Street**. Stop to take photos at the ❸ **Daily Telegraph Building**. Turn around almost at the end of Tennyson Street pass the attractive **Masonic Hotel**, before you look in the ❹ **Art Deco Shop** *(daily 9am–5pm | 7 Tennyson Street)* opposite and admire the Art Deco collection of knick-knacks, hats and books. **Cross the Marine Parade, then turn left on a wonderful cycle route** along the waterside, past

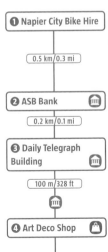

❶ Napier City Bike Hire

0.5 km/0.3 mi

❷ ASB Bank

0.2 km/0.1 mi

❸ Daily Telegraph Building

100 m/328 ft

❹ Art Deco Shop

A small tower with a giant view of the sunrise: Nugget Point in the Catlins

0.5 km/0.3 mi

5 Pania of the Reef

4.3 km/2.7 mi

6 Shed 2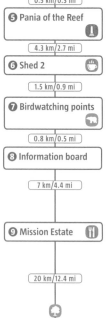

1.5 km/0.9 mi

7 Birdwatching points

0.8 km/0.5 mi

8 Information board

7 km/4.4 mi

9 Mission Estate

20 km/12.4 mi

5 **Pania of the Reef**, the sculpture of a Maori mermaid. **From here, simply follow the signs for the Napier City Loop,** cycle through the busy harbour district of Ahuriri where after 4 km/2.5 mi you can stop for coffee in the original **6** Shed 2 *(1 Lever Street | shed2.co.nz)*.

01:00pm **Then, follow the cycle route over the bridge**, head through the wetland with many local birds that you can see from two **7** **birdwatching points**. **Then, turn around and head left onto the Embankment Road and head straight on to the Ahuriri Estuary Walk**, past an **8** **information board** with interesting facts about the earthquake in 1931. The landscape becomes more rural, on the left are fields and on the right the canal. After about 15 km/9.3 mi the first vineyards come into view, and so you don't fall off the saddle, treat yourself to a light snack accompanied by an excellent wine in the pleasant **9** **Mission Estate** *(198 Church Street | missionestate.co.nz | Moderate)*. You will have to opt out of the wine tasting, as you still have half of the route ahead of you...

03:00pm **Continue cycling on the Napier City Trail** through the heart of the rural small town. Now, you will make some progress. In Riverside Park, you head through green river meadows along the Tutaekuri River and endless vines until you arrive at the sea again where **Cape Kidnappers → p. 52** and its white sandstone cliffs glint in the distance. If you're lucky, with a tail wind you will travel by the waterside to the ⑩ **New Zealand National Aquarium** *(daily 9am–5pm | NZ$21 | 546 Marine Parade | www. nationalaquarium.co.nz)*, where you can admire everything that thrives to your right in the sea. From here, you will quickly arrive – **continue straight ahead by the sea** – at your staring point at ❶ **Napier City Bike Hire**, where you can hand back the bikes.

⑩ New Zealand
National Aquarium

1.2 km / 0.7 mi

❶ Napier City Bike Hire

4 WILDLIFE TOUR THROUGH THE CATLINS

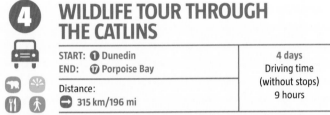

START: ❶ Dunedin	4 days
END: ⑰ Porpoise Bay	Driving time (without stops) 9 hours
Distance: ➡ 315 km/196 mi	

COSTS: approx. NZ$1,350 for 2 people (accommodation, food, hire car, petrol, surfing course, kayak tour)
WHAT TO PACK: binoculars, outdoor wear

IMPORTANT TIPS: Seals can move surprisingly quickly on land. Maintain the required safety distance and never block the route to the sea! Penguins also feel easily disturbed, if you get too close.
Access to the ⑭ Cathedral Caves is only possible at low tide.

On New Zealand's southern tip, in the secluded bays of the Catlins, close to the bottom of the world, animals (not humans) rule the beaches: seals defend their territory, Hector's dolphins swim with the waves and in the twilight penguins waddle out of the sea. An intense experience of wild nature is on hikes, kayak tours and riding the waves.

From ❶ **Dunedin**, **head south.** In the early afternoon, you reach the coastal town of ❷ **Kaka Point.** Check into your **crib**, as the Kiwis call their simple, reasonably priced holiday homes, for two nights, e.g. **Campbell Reef Cottage** *(kakapointholidayhomes.co.nz)* or **Nugget Lodge** *(nuggetlodge.co.nz)* by the sea or on the cliffs by the beach. Then, make a detour to ❸ **Roaring Bay a little further south.** From shelters you can observe yellow-eyed

DAY 1

❶ Dunedin

100 km / 62 mi

❷ Kaka Point

9 km / 5.6 mi

❸ Roaring Bay

8 km / 5 mi

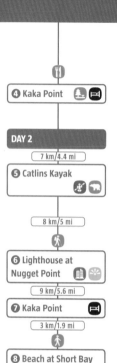

④ Kaka Point

DAY 2

7 km/4.4 mi

⑤ Catlins Kayak

8 km/5 mi

⑥ Lighthouse at Nugget Point

9 km/5.6 mi

⑦ Kaka Point

3 km/1.9 mi

⑧ Beach at Short Bay

DAY 3

36 km/22.4 mi

⑨ Purakaunui Bay

11 km/6.8 mi

⑩ Purakaunui Falls

17 km/10.6 mi

⑪ Papatowai

6 km/3.7 mi

⑫ Lake Wilkie

29 km/18 mi

⑬ Mohua Park

penguins that hop out of the sea at twilight. Find out about the latest tides by phoning the **Catlins Info Center** *(tel. 03 415 83 71 | catlins.org.nz)*. Back in ④ **Kaka Point** there is fish & chips with freshly caught blue cod at **The Point Café** *(daily 9am–6pm | 58 Esplanade)*. Take your food to the beach and eat it here at one of the wooden tables.

Next morning, meet **at the Fishing Camp on the beach at Nuggets Road**. If the sea is calm, you can head out with guide Jared Anderson from ⑤ INSIDER TIP **Catlins Kayak** *(2.5 hr-tour NZ$125 | Nuggets Road | tel. 027 416 49 11 | cat linskayak.co.nz)* to a **seal colony** with over 500 animals on the cliffs below the lighthouse at Nugget Point. If you're lucky, albatrosses soar above your head, or rare elephant seals appear near the boat. Afterwards, **drive five minutes in the car from Fishing Camp to a hill above the sea, and hike from the car park along the cliffs to the** ⑥ **lighthouse at Nugget Point**. Look at the cliffs (nuggets) dotted in the sea from above. Prepare your dinner at your crib in ⑦ **Kaka Point**, as apart from fish & chips the town has no other restaurants. Before it gets dark, there is still time for a solitary walk to the ⑧ **beach at Short Bay**, which is full of driftwood **on the 10 km/6.2 mi coast road between Kaka Point and Nugget Point.** Not much nightlife goes on here, but you can marvel at the universe on your own under the twinkling starry sky.

Next day, **head south for** ⑨ INSIDER TIP **Purakaunui Bay**. Here, nature is your vast cinema: the lonely bay is dominated by seals, and surrounded by high cliffs and dunes. This makes swimming in the surf a real adventure. **A few minutes by car inland the** ⑩ **Purakaunui Falls** cascade 20 m/65.6 ft into the dense rainforest. **You can walk to the waterfalls from a car park in about ten minutes.** Back on the coast in ⑪ **Papatowai** admire the **Lost Gypsy Gallery** *(Thu–Tue 10am–5pm | Papatowai Highway | thelost gypsy.com)* in a converted bus – on show are the quirky artworks by Blair Somerville made from driftwood, mussels and wire. **Along the Southern Scenic Route you carry on to Tautuku. From here, hike around the reflecting** ⑫ **Lake Wilkie**, which is surrounded by up to 50 m/164 ft tall podocarp trees. In the evening, **head back inland** to the eco retreat ⑬ **Mohua Park** *(4 rooms | 744 Catlins Valley Road | tel. 03 415 86 13 | catlinsmohuapark.co.nz | Moderate)* in Tawanui, where you stay overnight in luxury cottages with a view over the Catlins River Valley.

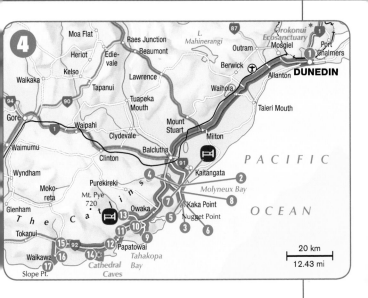

Before you go to sleep you should definitely try one of the **Bush Walks** *(approx. 20 min)* into the rainforest on your doorstep! In the dense greenery, New Zealand is still alive as it was in the days of the first Maoris: *Wood pigeons* fly through giant ferns, and between branches overgrown with moss over 1,000-year-old *Matai Trees* soar upwards like giant pillars.

After breakfast, head for the ⑭ **Cathedral Caves**, 30 m/ 98.4 ft high rocky caves on Waipati Beach. **A long path (1 km/0.6 mi) leads from the car park to the beach.** The caves are only accessible at low tide! At lunchtime you can head for the ⑮ **Niagara Falls Café** *(daily 10am–5pm | 256 Niagara-Waikawa Road | tel. 03 2 46 85 77 | niagarafallscafe.co.nz | Budget)* in Niagara. The speciality is smoked salmon from Stewart Island – otherwise, only local ingredients are used. The next stop is ⑯ **Curio Bay**. At low tide, the remains of a 180-million-year-old fossilized forest are exposed – the **Jurassic Petrified Forest** – and yellow-eyed penguins often appear. ⑰ **Porpoise Bay nearby** is ideal for surfing beginners *(Catlins Surf | 2 hr surf course incl. board and wet-suit NZ$60 | catlins-surf.co.nz)*. If you manage to stay upright on the board and Hector's dolphins dive in the water next to you, your Catlins Trip was perfect!

DAY 4

37 km / 23 mi

⑭ Cathedral Caves

26 km / 15.2 mi

⑮ Niagara Falls Café

9 km / 5.6 mi

⑯ Curio Bay

2 km / 1.2 mi

⑰ Porpoise Bay

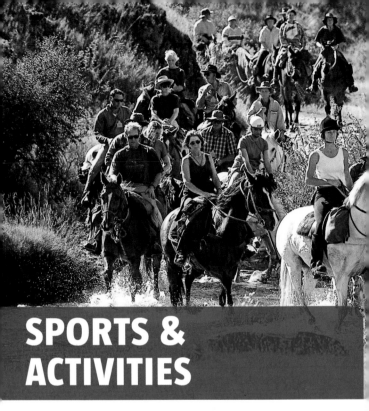

SPORTS & ACTIVITIES

Kiwis are basically sporting mad and that can be infectious. Take the plunge with the water sports of accessory of your choice, climb mountains or conquer New Zealand's nature by bicycle.

ADVENTURE SPORTS

The steepest, fastest or craziest! Superlatives apply for everything in the native home of the bungy jump. Popular centres for this adrenalin rush are in the north in Rotorua and Taupo, in the south around Queenstown and Wanaka. *Jet Boats (tel. 0800 32 78 53 | www.dart river.co.nz)* glide over the turquoise-coloured Dart River near Glenorchy. Or climb the rock faces – with *Wanaka Rock Climbing (tel. 022 015 44 58 | www.wanakarock.*

co.nz) for beginners and pros. Keep your eyes open during *Tandem Paragliding (tel. 0800 58 67 66 | skydivetaupo.co.nz)* over Taupo, as the panoramic views are incredible! If you prefer to float above the earth, try *Freefall Extreme (tel. 0800 94 98 88 | velocityvalley.co.nz)* in Rotorua above a 220 km/h/137 mph wind tunnel. As preparation you can attend *Survival Training (tel. 0800 78 78 48 | www.sossurvivaltraining. com)* in the wilderness around Auckland.

CYCLING

An excellent cycle route network extends from New Zealand's mountainous north as far as the south; full information is available on *www.nzcycletrail.com*. You can enjoy one- and multi-day tours with

The world's most thrilling sports arena offers challenges on land, sea and in the air – a test for die-hard and aspiring adventurers

Natural High (tel. 09 257 46 73 | www.naturalhigh.co.nz): with a support bus you only ride on the most picturesque parts of the trail. Or, 150 km/93 mi along an old train track on the *Otago Central Rail Trail (www.otagorailtrail.co.nz)*, past a historic gold rush town and never-ending South Island panoramic views. Mountain bikers can test all their skills, *www.ridenz.co* lists countless trails: the legendary ⚡ *42 Traverse* e.g. is an undulating trail for 46 km/28.6 mi through the forest and bush with views of North Island's volcanoes. The challenging ⚡ *Old Ghost Trail (oldghostroad.org.nz)* along the wild west coast in the south is the country's longest trail and only suitable for the fearless. Fans of the MTB course can test their skills on the *FourForty (www.fourfortymtbpark.co.nz)* in Auckland and in the *Cardrona Bike Park (cardrona.com)* as well as on trails in the mountains around Queenstown. More information is available at *www.ridenz.co*. In New Zealand, you are required to wear a helmet. And always ride on the left!

HIKING

You must register for all nine *Great Walks* with the Department of Conservation *(doc.govt.nz/great-walks)* and book the huts in advance. In particular, the *Milford Track* is usually fully booked months ahead. If you prefer marathon hiking, you can trek across the entire country from north to south on the 3,000 km/1,864 mi long and well-integrated *Te Araroa – New Zealand's Trail (www.teararoa.org.nz)*. There are shorter hiking trails around the country; these are listed by North- or South Island or by name on *www.freewalks.nz*.

HORSERIDING

Horseriding through breathtaking countryside is available for beginners and experienced riders countrywide. You can gallop with *Ahipara Horse Treks (tel. 09 408 25 32 | www.taitokerauhoney.co.nz)* across Ninety Mile Beach in Northland or across the bright white sand of Pakiri Beach *(tel. 09 422 62 75 | www.horseride-nz.co.nz)* north of Auckland. In the impressive setting of mountains and lakes around Queenstown *(tel. 0800 23 65 66 | nzhorsetreks. co.nz)* you can enjoy fabulous views from horseback. Horse safaris off the beaten track that last for several days are available with *Alpine Horse Safaris (www. alpinehorse.co.nz)* in Canterbury. More information: *truenz.co.nz/horsetrekking*

KAJAK & CANOEING

Tranquil lakes, fast-flowing rivers and a diverse sea coast offer fans of paddle sports ideal conditions almost throughout the country and in the national parks. On a **INSIDER TIP** canoe tour through *Pelorus Sound (canoe hire in Elaine Bay from NZ$60 | tel. 03 576 52 51 | seakaya*

kingmarlborough.co.nz) on the northern tip of South Island you escape civilization after a few strokes of the paddle and travel along unspoilt, secluded bays. You will use every muscle during a *kayak excursion (tel. 0800 99 90 89 | aucklandseak ayaks.co.nz)* in Hauraki Gulf to Rangitoto and while climbing the volcano.

KITE- & WINDSURFING

Two oceans close together, high mountains, rapidly changing weather: New Zealand is a paradise for wind sports fanatics. You can learn kite- and windsurfing on the northern tip of South Island in *Nelson (tel. 0800 548 326 | www.kite scool.co.nz)* and in *Auckland (tel. 09 815 06 83 | nzboardstore.co.nz)* – with a west wind in Point Chevalier, or with an east wind Orewa is popular. *www.windsurfingnz.org, Facebook: new zealand kitesurfing*

SAILING

A good breeze is always blowing in the *Bay of Islands* and naturally: in the City of Sails – Auckland. If you want to feel the air at the America's Cup, you can tame the winds in Auckland on one of the high-tech boats sailing at speed *(tel. 0800 39 75 67 | www.exploregroup.co.nz)*. An *Akaroa Sailing Cruise (tel. 0800 72 45 28 | aclasssailing.co.nz)* near Christchurch is a much gentler pace.

SKIING

In New Zealand's winter sports centres there is snow from June to September. In the north around the volcano *Ruapehu* are the ski areas *Whakapapa* and *Turoa*. Ski hype is on the agenda – also for snowboard fans and heli skiers – in Queenstown *(www.queenstownnz.co.nz)*

with the arenas at *Coronet Peak*, *Treble Cone*, *Cardrona* and *The Remarkables*.
INSIDER TIP *Soho Basin (tel. 03 450 90 98 | sohobasin.com)* near Cardrona is exclusive: a snow crawler or helicopter transports you to the slopes with untouched powdery snow. Over the mountain next door in Wanaka, you will find New Zealand's only cross-country ski run *(snow farmnz.com)* and near Christchurch a handful of cute slopes on *Mount Hutt*.

SUP & SURFING

In New Zealand, surfing is a lifestyle; riding the waves on stand-up paddle boards (SUP) is also becoming increasingly popular. Most of the surfing hotspots are on North Island and generally the east is tamer than the west. Popular surfing spots with boards for hire are *Piha* and *Muriwai* on Auckland's west coast, a little further south *Raglan* and along the *Surf Highway (SH 45)* in Taranaki. The top surfing spots on the east coast are in Northland around *Mangawhai* and in *Gisborne*. In the chilly south, among the favourites are *Sumner* in Christchurch and *St Clair* in Dunedin. Updated surfing weather forecasts are at *marineweath er.co.nz* or *magicseaweed.com*. A tranquil SUP tour is possible in the protected bays and on many lakes, for example, *Lake Rotoiti* near Rotorua, the *Tutukaka Coast* or *Raglan Harbour*.

WELLNESS

In the country of thermal springs there are plenty of hot pools; an overview is at *www.nzhotpools.co.nz*. At Lewis Pass *Maruia Hot Springs (SH7 | tel. 03 5 23 88 40 | www.maruiahotsprings.nz)*. is a wellness oasis away from mass tourism. If you have the resources, you can get some pampering in the luxury wellness and spa retreats in a secluded part of nature – e.g. on the edge of the Abel Tasman National Park, on Tutukaka Coast, in the middle of the forest near Rotorua or on Lake Pukaki with views of Mount Cook – from the hot tub. Detailed information at *www.newzealand. com*, key word wellness or spa retreat.

Exciting bike tours are offered in many places.

TRAVEL WITH KIDS

Without being afraid of dangerous animals, in New Zealand the kids can feel like explorers: panning gold dust from rivers, running across swaying swing bridges and watching seals surfing among the waves.

There is a slight risk only from the sun's strong rays, traffic on the left and beaches with dangerous currents (and rarely visited by sharks). It's essential to wear a sun hat and sunscreen with high UV protection factor. Every young Kiwi also knows that you should only swim on the beach within the marker flags that are monitored by the lifeguards. It's masses of fun, if you have a body board to ride the waves. They are usually available cheaply in second-hand shops that you find in New Zealand in every small town – just like other toys that you cannot bring with you from home.

You can impress your kids if you book overnight stays in farmhouses *(e.g. Kauri Tree Hut | Mangawhaicano pycamping.co.nz/kauri-tree-hut | Expensive)*, in candy-coloured retro caravans *(Claris | near Maraetai | www.booka bach.co.nz | Budget)*, Mongolian yurts *(e.g. Wacky Stays | Kaikourawackystays. co.nz | Moderate)* or the *Hobbit Motel (www.waitomomotel.co.nz | Moderate)* in Waitomo. Camper vans sleeping up to six are suitable for large families. When booking you should check that there is enough space for children's seats. A good alternative are cabins on camping grounds or typical New Zealand cribs,

Counting rainbows, wading through secluded rivers and gathering mussels from rocks – in New Zealand the best things are for free

as the Kiwis call their holiday houses (*www.bookabach.co.nz, www.holiday houses.co.nz*). Most have children's rooms with bunk beds and shelves of board games.

If you're feeling confident: bungy jumping e.g. in *Adventure Park Velocity Valley* in Rotorua is allowed from age of ten (the minimum weight is 35 kg/77 lbs). Great fun are also the A & P Agricultural Shows that take place across the country in the summer. At these shows, farmers parade their sheep and cows;

there are lumbering competitions and bouncy castles for the kids and mostly soft ice cream from Mr Whippy as well as hot dogs on a stick – two typical New Zealand treats for children. The same goes for fluffies, milk froth with mini-marshmallows in mini-cups that children often get for free in cafés when their parents order coffee. You notice how much Kiwis love children by the high-chairs and play niches in every restaurant – and almost on every beach or river somebody has fixed a tyre swing to a tree. If your child should get bored while travelling, you are guaranteed to find a meadow close by with sheep that the kids can stroke!

NORTH ISLAND

DUNE SURFING (150 B1) *(ⓜ F2)*
The perfect picture for the photo album: when the entire family plunges together on body boards into the

KELLY TARLTON'S SEALIFE AQUARIUM (152 B1–2) *(ⓜ H–J5)*
What's lurking in the Pacific? Plexiglass tunnels lead through aquariums with 1,500 sea creatures, including sharks and turtles. In the Antarctic department, penguins from the South Pole even waddle through the snow. *Daily 9.30am–5pm | adults NZ$39, children over three years NZ$27, under age of three free | 23 Tamaki Drive | Auckland | www.kellytarltons.co.nz*

Let's do a lap – with Hector's dolphins. Brilliant for young swimmers!

100 m/328 ft high dunes in the dune landscape in Te Paki on Cape Reinga, the conditions are ideal. It's best to bring your own boards or you can hire them on location for approx. NZ$15.

KIWI HOUSE (152 B4) *(ⓜ J6)*
Kiwis rarely appear in the wild. They usually emerge at night time in the bush. At the Kiwi House in the small town of Otorohanga, the kids can also see the

TRAVEL WITH KIDS

timid birds. In the breeding station, everything focuses on the animals' survival, so kiwi chicks are not a rare sight. *Daily 9am–5pm | adults NZ$24, children over 5 years NZ$8 | 20 Alex Telfer Drive | kiwihouse.org.nz*

LAMA TREKKING (152 B4) (*Ⅲ J7*)
A good trick to inspire the kids to go hiking: trekking with lamas; they carry the luggage and look cute. The guided tours through King Country last between two hours and a full day and are near Piopio on the west coast with *Greenmount Llamas. 2 hr tour adults NZ$100, children NZ$80, ½ day adults NZ$150, children NZ$130 | 142 Paekaka Road | tel. 07 8 77 82 97 | www.greenmountllamas.co.nz*

WETA WORKSHOP STUDIOS ●
(155 D5) (*Ⅲ H10*)
Life-size models and original props from films like "The Hobbit", "King Kong" or "Lord of the Rings". During a 45-minute tour of the Oscar-winning studio for special effects and costume design in Wellington, kids and adults get a great visual show of how to animate fantasy characters on the computer. *Adults NZ$25, children NZ$12, book tickets online in advance | Weka Street/corner of Camperdown Road | www.wetaworkshop.com*

SOUTH ISLAND

DOLPHIN CRUISE (157 E–F2) (*Ⅲ H10*)
Swimming with dolphins is particularly safe in the calm waters of the Marlborough Sounds. But it's also enough to watch the jumping Bottlenose- and Hector's dolphins from the boat, (children are only allowed in the water aged over eight years). *E-Ko Tours start in Picton. Adults NZ$99, children over five years NZ$55; boat tour + swimming with dolphins: adults NZ$165, children NZ$135 |*

1 Wellington Street | tel. 03 5 73 80 40 | www.e-ko.nz

INSIDER TIP ► MARGARET MAHY PLAYGROUND (157 D5) (*Ⅲ F13*)
On the biggest playground of the southern hemisphere on the Avon River in Christchurch, the kids can play for hours: trampolining, aerial cable car or hopping in the fountains. There are even talking toilets! *177 Armagh Street*

NATIONAL TRANSPORT AND TOY MUSEUM (159 D2) (*Ⅲ C14–15*)
At last a museum which is fun for the whole family: at the National Transport and Toy Museum in Wanaka adults can admire old aircraft and old-timers (e.g. 1930s Chevrolets), while the kids look at New Zealand's biggest Barbie collection and over 1,000 Star Wars figures. Don't miss the toy shop at the end! *Daily 8.30am–5pm | adults NZ$18, children NZ$5 | 891 Wanaka-Luggate Highway | nttmuseumwanaka.co.nz*

SHANTYTOWN (156 B4) (*Ⅲ E12*)
Enjoy a nostalgia trip to the year 1860: in the reconstructed gold rush town, children can wash gold, travel on a steam locomotive through the rainforest or have their photos taken in historic costumes. South of Greymouth. *Daily 8.30am–5pm | adults NZ$33, children over five years NZ$16 | 316 Rutherglen Road | www.shantytown.co.nz*

SKYLINE LUGE QUEENSTOWN ☼
(158 C3) (*Ⅲ C15*)
Take a Gondola ride up the mountain and then race back down again with a luge ride and enjoy the panoramic view over Queenstown: a luge ride is almost as much fun as sledging – adults can also enjoy it. *Daily from 10am | 5 rides incl. gondola ride adults NZ$55, children over five years NZ$45 | www.skyline.co.nz*

FESTIVALS & EVENTS

The Kiwis are good at partying and they love it! Whether it's a public holiday, festival or sports event: any excuse is fine here. If the national holiday falls on a weekend, everyone gets Monday off in lieu. In winter, everything stops, and the Kiwis go into hibernation. But in the winter sports centre of Queenstown it's getting busy!

FESTIVALS & EVENTS

JANUARY
Glenorchy Race Day: serious horse races with rodeo and a folk fest atmosphere at the north end of Lake Wakatipu. *glenorchyinfocentre.co.nz*

FEBRUARY
Splore: Music festival in a beguiling coastal location south of Auckland. Three days to rock with a dress up day and camping at the festival site. *www.splore.net*

MARCH
Wildfoods Festival: a folk festival for gluttony with adventurous delicacies like Huhu worm sushi in Hokitika on the west coast. *wildfoods.co.nz*
WOMAD: Music, dance and art with a hippie atmosphere – international, three-day music festival in New Plymouth. Totally child-friendly. *www.womad.co.nz*

INSIDER **TIP** ▶ *Dragonboat Festival:* Dragon boat drama with school and business teams in early March in Wellington Harbour. *dragonboatfestival.co.nz*

MARCH/APRIL
Wairarapa Balloon Festival: Hot-air balloon spectacle north of Wellington with a mass start at sunrise and *Night Glow*, where the balloons are tethered on the ground and light up the night sky. Always over Easter. *www.nzballoons.co.nz*

APRIL
Graperide: Bike ride with wine tasting over a 101 km/63 mi beautiful, hair-raising route in Marlborough. *graperide.co.nz*

JUNE
Wellington Jazzfestival: The small capital with a big reputation for jazz music – three days with hundreds of musicians. *jazzfestival.co.nz*
Matariki: The Maori New Year with numerous cultural events countrywide. *www.matarikifestival.org.nz*

Wine tasting, eating worms, cheering bands: New Zealanders prefer to party outdoors – with plenty of music and garish costumes

AUGUST
Winter Games: At this 14-day event, numerous international winter sports stars appear in Queenstown. *winter gamesnz.kiwi*

SEPTEMBER
WOW World of Wearable Art: This event is not only a creative fashion show of the most innovative and eye-catching costumes but also a design competition in Wellington. *www.world ofwearableart.com*

OCTOBER
French Fest Akaroa: Small fest organized by the idiosyncratic French community with waiter/waitress races and baguettes as a baton *(Facebook: French Fest Akaroa)*.

DECEMBER
Festival month with concerts across the country and during the New Zealand summer holidays

Rhythm & Vines: Legendary, multi-day music festival in the vineyards of Gisborne. Party until the world's first sunrise of the new year.

Rhythm & Alps: The sister event in the mountains in Cardrona Valley in Wanaka. *www.rhythmandalps.co.nz*

PUBLIC HOLIDAYS

1 Jan	New Year
6 Feb	Waitangi Day
March/April	Good Friday/ Easter Monday
25 April	ANZAC Day (Remembrance day for servicemen and women)
1st Mon in June	Queen's Birthday
4th Mon in Oct	Labour Weekend
25 Dec	Christmas Day
26 Dec	Boxing Day

LINKS, BLOGS, APPS & MORE

ecofind.co.nz Are you looking for organic restaurants, eco lodges or sustainable and fair trade products? This website helps you travel around New Zealand as eco-friendly as possible.

undertheradar.co.nz Concerts, festivals and interviews with musicians. The best resource to learn about New Zealand's music scene and gigs with international stars

maorimaps.com Maps listing all the *Marae* (public assembly houses of the Maori communities) – with local addresses, in case you plan to visit one of the meeting houses decorated with traditional wood carvings

backpackerguide.nz A very useful web portal for everyone touring New Zealand with a backpack, incl. information about hostels, jobs or buying a car

grabone.co.nz Cheap deals for outdoor activities, restaurants, hotels and spa treatments throughout New Zealand

stuff.co.nz What are the top news stories in New Zealand? If you want to have a say, stay up to date on New Zealand's best news website – and receive updated travel tips

Breadcrumbs.nz Top tips for surfing spots, hidden waterfalls and craft beer bars: at Breadcrumbs, users rec-

Regardless of whether you are still researching your trip or already in New Zealand: these addresses will provide you with more information, videos and networks to make your holiday even more enjoyable

ommend their favourite places in New Zealand. With no rating system, but like a tip from a good friend. That's how you discover the places, you'd otherwise never find

jellyjourneys.com Get in the mood for New Zealand: professionally made videos by two travel Vloggers from England who film themselves river rafting, sailing or riding in a hot-air balloon in the "land of the long white cloud"

countingthebeat.gen.nz New Zealand music podcast dedicated to the Kiwis' versatile music scene. Every podcast is about a different genre, and all the songs are played on a record player. Broadcast on Waiheke Radio

tvnz.co.nz On New Zealand's TV website you find plenty of films and up-to-date travel documentaries

Camper Mate Really useful App with digital maps that function offline and lists of all the country's camping grounds. Information about prices, sanitary facilities and wastewater sites is constantly updated. Booking camping sites is also possible with the App

Met Service The weather can rapidly change in New Zealand. With the App from New Zealand's Meteorological Service you're always kept updated about the rain, sun and storm forecasts

Star Chart Not familiar with the stars in the southern hemisphere? Then you can trust this App

TRAVEL TIPS

ACCOMMODATION

You will find a wide choice of holiday houses at *www.bookabach.co.nz* and *www.holidayhouses.co.nz*. If you are travelling in a camper van or with a tent, there are several kinds of camp grounds. There are privately run camp sites, which offer shared kitchens and often comfortable huts for several people *(camping pitch approx. NZ$20/person | nzcamping.com)*. About 200 camping grounds managed by the Department of Conservation (DOC) are considerably cheaper and located in remote places in the great outdoors *(from NZ$8/person)*. Facilities vary – serviced camp sites with cooking bench, hot showers and toilets can be reserved with the relevant DOC Visitor Centre for the region. Camp sites in the categories scenic, standard and basic generally have non-flushing toilets and a water tap with cold water and cannot be reserved in advance (they are cheaper, and occasionally free of charge). Information at *www.doc.govt.nz*.

Freedom Camping grounds are free of charge throughout the country; however, these can only be used by camper vans with a flush toilet and wastewater tank. Information at *www.freedomcamping.org*. The App *Campermate* is especially helpful and provides exact details about the facilities at the camp sites and wastewater facilities in the area. Unique cabins and glamping tents in the wilderness are offered by *Canopy Camping (www.canopycamping.co.nz)*. Hotels, motels and B&Bs are listed e.g. on *www.booking.com*, *www.wotif.co.nz* or *www.bnb.co.nz*. Backpackers can find lodgings at *www.yha.co.nz*, *www.bbh.co.nz* or *www.backpackerguide.nz*. You will find a wide selection of boutique hotels in historical buildings at *www.heritageinns.co.nz*.

RESPONSIBLE TRAVEL

It doesn't take a lot to be environmentally friendly whilst travelling. Don't just think about your carbon footprint whilst flying to and from your holiday destination but also about how you can protect nature and culture abroad. As a tourist it is especially important to respect nature, look out for local products, cycle instead of driving, save water and much more. If you would like to find out more about eco-tourism please visit: *www.ecotourism.org*

ARRIVAL

Travel from the left or right? You reach New Zealand from both directions around the globe. Depending on the route, the flight time is about 24 hours. If you prefer, you can also turn your arrival and departure into a world trip. *Air New Zealand (www.airnewzealand.com)* offers flights via Asia and returning via the US. When you book, you can decide where you want to break your journey. For example, in Singapore, L.A. or on the Pacific Islands. Tip: in the airline's Premium Economy class you travel just as comfortably as in Business Class. Depending on availability, at the check-in you can purchase a twin seat in the regular Economy Class for about NZ$100, which guarantees that the seat next to you remains free (not available on all flights). If you want to stretch out during the flight, book a Skycouch in Economy Class: a seating row with three seats that transforms into a couch with folding legs; two people can recline next to each other (from NZ$1,200 per couple/on the route London–Los Angeles–Auckland). With *Emirates (www.emirates.com)* you first fly to Dubai (6.5 hr) and from here in about 17 hours with a stopover in Australia (e.g. Sydney or Melbourne) to New Zealand. You can enjoy the airline's on-board entertainment with plenty of films and games. The journey with *Singapore Airlines (www.singaporeair.com)* is pleasant with a stopover in Singapore. Plenty of leg room is available with *Qatar Airways (www.qatarairways.com)* in the Economy Class on flights to Auckland. After a stop in Doha (often with free overnight hotel accommodation) you continue on the world's longest flight (16.5 hr) across ten time zones to New Zealand. In short: you have found a cheap flight from Europe, if you pay between £1,000 and £1,300 for a return trip in Economy Class. You will get return trips from the US east coast for about US$1,000, from the west coast prices are significantly lower.

CAR & CAMPERVAN HIRE

Generally, you must be at least 21 years of age to hire a car. If you plan to hire a car: a medium-class car costs approx. NZ$70/day e.g. with *Europcar (www.europcar.co.nz)*. or *GoRentals (www.gorentals.co.nz)*. You should book your camper van several months before your flight, if possible, because demand is particularly high in summer. Then, a day in the camper may already be more expensive than the combination of hotel and hire car (often more than NZ$300/day). *EuroCamper (eurocamper.co.nz)* and *Wendekreisen (www.wendekreisen.co.nz)* offer fair prices. A kind of Airbnb for owners of campers is *Share A Camper (www.shareacamper.com)*; they rent out their private vehicles. *Nomad Campervans (www.nomadnz.com)* specializes in VW camper vans. The size of camper vans ranges from smaller hi-top campers for 2–3 people to camper vans with six beds. When booking a camper van, you should make sure it is certified as "self-contained" – i.e. your vehicle has a toilet and wastewater tank. This is essential if you plan to stay overnight at the *Freedom Campsites* which are free of charge. If you cannot do without the Internet while travelling, some rental companies also offer the option to book a camper with WiFi on board.

CLIMATE, WHEN TO GO

Two narrow islands in the middle of the sea at the bottom of the world: it's not surprising that New Zealand is exposed to the vagaries of the ocean. You should be prepared – even in summer (Dec–Feb) – for sudden weather changes. You should definitely pack rainwear, a hat and down jacket (especially when you are travelling on South Island). The climate in the north of North Island is sub-tropical and in the south comparable with Central Europe. The best time to travel is during New Zealand's summer. Winter in New Zealand begins in May/June and ends in October. The skiing season on North- and South Island lasts from July to September.

CURRENCY CONVERTER

£	NZ$	NZ$	£
1	1.94	10	5.16
2	3.88	20	10.32
3	5.82	25	12.90
5	9.70	50	25.80
7	13.58	75	38.70
10	19.40	100	51.60
15	29.10	125	64.50
25	48.50	150	77.40
50	97	200	103.20

US$	NZ$	NZ$	US$
1	1.48	10	6.75
2	2.96	20	13.50
3	4.44	25	16.88
5	7.40	50	33.75
7	10.36	75	50.63
10	14.80	100	67.50
15	22.20	125	84.38
25	37	150	101.25
50	74	200	135

For current exchange rates see www.xe.com

CONSULATES AND EMBASSIES

BRITISH HIGH COMMISSION
44 Hill Street | Wellington 6011 | tel. +46 4 924 2888 | ukinnewzealand.fco. gov.uk

CONSULATE GENERAL OF THE US
3rd Floor 23, Citigroup Building | Customs Street E (cnr. Commerce Street) | Auckland 1010| tel. +64 4 462 6000 | nz.usembassy.gov

HIGH COMMISSION OF CANADA
Level 11, 125 The Terrace | Wellington 6011 | tel. +64 4 473 9577 | www.canada international.gc.ca/new_zealand-nou velle_zelande

CUSTOMS

You are allowed to import e.g. 4.5 l wine and 50 cigarettes (per person). To protect New Zealand's flora and fauna you must declare foodstuffs, plants, seeds and animal products on entry. Camping equipment and hiking boots, which are still muddy, must also be declared. If you are returning to the EU, you are permitted to carry e.g. 200 cigarettes, 4 l wine and gifts up to a value of £390. US residents get information on custom regulations at *www.cbp.gov*.

DRIVING

In New Zealand the traffic drives on the left. You should therefore look right when travelling on a roundabout. Information about the most important traffic rules is at *drivesafe.org.nz*.
Journeys often take longer than expected in New Zealand because there is generally two-way traffic. You should plan more time or calculate your route using the route planner on the official New Zealand website *www.new zealand.com*. On highways, the maximum speed is 100 km/h/62 mph and in towns 50 km/h/31 mph. Mobile telephones are banned while driving; you should never drive with more than 0.5 per mill alcohol in the blood. You require an international driving licence to drive on the roads.
If you wish to buy a car to get around in New Zealand: you can find used cars on the online platform *www.trademe.co.nz* or at the *Ellerslie Car Fair (every Sun*

9am–noon | Ellerslie Racecourse | car fair.co.nz) in Auckland.

ELECTRICITY

Mains voltage is 230/240 Volt. You can find an adapter for the three-pin flat plug at the airport, at petrol stations on in shops like The Warehouse.

HEALTH

You are recommended to have the standard vaccinations before your trip. New Zealand has a very good healthcare system. Tourists are also entitled to free first aid treatment in case of an accident *(accident compensation)*. You should organize a good travel insurance policy incl. return travel in case of an emergency.

IMMIGRATION

Your passport must be valid on arrival for at least another month after the intended duration of your stay. You don't need a visa for a visit of up to three months in New Zealand. If you want to stay for up to twelve months, you can apply for a visa online *(www.immigration.govt.nz)*. Important note: for a stopover in the USA, you require an electronic passport and must apply for your ESTA authorization before you start your trip. If you are planning a stop in Asia, your passport should be valid for at least six months. A "Working Holiday" visa *(www.workingholidaynewzealand.com)* entitles you to work for one year and you can apply for this from the immigration authorities. Applicants should not be aged over 30 years. Provisionally, from mid-2019 two new regulations apply for tourists. On the one

hand, visitors from overseas must apply online for an Electronic Travel Authority (ETA) (valid for 2 years). This will cost between NZ$9 and NZ$12.50 per person. On the other hand, every international visitor should pay a *levy*

BUDGETING

Coffee	£2.60/US$3.40 *for a flat white*
Souvenirs	£13/US$17 *for a pair of merino woollen socks*
Wine	£8/US$10 *for one bottle*
Bacon & Eggs	£8/US$10 *for one portion*
Petrol	£1.12/US$1.47 *for one litre super*
Intercity-Bus	£26/US$34 *Auckland–Wellington one way*

of approx. NZ$35 to maintain the tourist infrastructure and protect the environment. ETAs and the *levy* can be paid for online before your arrival. More information: *www.mbie.govt.nz/border-changes*

INFORMATION

100 % Pure New Zealand (www.newzealand.com), New Zealand's official tourism and travel website provides information about all the country's destinations and offers plenty of tips for travel around the country.

INTERNET & WIFI

The network coverage is good in all major towns and cities of the country.

However, usually in the wilderness you are not just remote from world events, but also cut off from the Internet.

A "WiFi for the back pocket" can be worthwhile, when there are no public hotspots: a prepaid-SIM card from *2degrees* with 1 GB of data is available for about NZ$20. With the *NZ Travel Card* from Spark for NZ$99 you get two months of up to 8 GB of data for example plus 1 GB daily, if you are in one of the country's over 1,000 *Free Spark WiFi Zones* (look out for the pink-coloured telephone boxes).

The Internet is now available free of charge in most accommodation, and also in libraries and most i-Sites (visitor information), plus in plenty of cafés you can get free Internet access. A country card with all free WiFi hotspots is available at wifispc.com.

MONEY & CREDIT CARDS

You can easily draw money with your credit card or EC card with Maestro logo from ATMs everywhere in the country (the charges depend on the respective bank). Visa- or MasterCard are accepted as a means of payment almost countrywide.

OPENING HOURS

Most shops are open Mon–Fri 9am–5pm and 11am–4pm on weekends. Big supermarket chains like Countdown, Pak 'n Save or New World are usually open all week until 10pm.

PHONE & MOBILE PHONE

There are four mobile phone providers in New Zealand: *Vodafone (www.voda*

WEATHER IN WELLINGON

	Jan.	Feb.	March	April	May	June	July	Aug.	Sept	Oct	Nov	Dec
Daytime temperatures in °C/°F	21/70	21/70	19/66	17/63	14/57	13/55	12/54	12/54	14/57	16/61	17/63	19/66
Night-time temperatures in °C/°F	13/55	13/55	12/54	11/52	8/46	7/45	6/43	6/43	8/46	9/48	10/50	12/54
Sunshine hours/day	8	7	6	5	4	4	4	4	6	6	7	7
Precipitation days/month	7	4	5	10	11	14	14	15	10	10	11	10
Water temperatures in °C/°F	17/63	18/64	18/64	17/63	14/57	14/57	13/55	13/55	12/54	14/57	14/57	17/63

☀ Sunshine hours/day 🌂 Precipitation days/month ≈ Water temperatures in °C/°F

fone.co.nz), *2Degrees (www.2degrees mobile.co.nz)*, *Spark (www.spark.co.nz)* and *Skinny (www.skinny.co.nz)*. All are available e.g. at The Warehouse, where you can insert a SIM card of the relevant provider in your mobile phone. You can now phone cheaply inside New Zealand, e.g. with the *NZ Travel Sim* from Spark for NZ\$29 monthly incl. 200 free minutes and 1 GB WiFi daily in one of more than 1,000 WiFi hotspots from Spark. If you want to make a phone call back home, it's worthwhile purchasing an *International Chat Pack (valid for one month)* from 2Degrees for NZ\$10 incl. 300 free minutes for phone calls to a landline. The country code for the United Kingdom from New Zealand is 0044, for the US and Cananda 001 and Australia 0061. To phone New Zealand: 0064. In case of an emergency, dial 111.

POST

The cost of a postcard to North America or Europe is NZ\$2.40 and it takes 6–10 working days. A letter costs NZ\$3.

TRANSPORT IN NEW ZEALAND

Air New Zealand (www.airnewzealand. com) and *Jetstar (www.jetstar.com)* offer domestic flights in New Zealand. A flight e.g. from Auckland to Christchurch costs between NZ\$100 and NZ\$150, depending on the travel time.
Long-distance trains only travel between Auckland and Wellington *(Northern Explorer)*, Christchurch and the west coast *(TranzAlpine)* or from Picton to Christchurch *(Coastal Pacific)*. Information and booking for everyone at *www.greatjourneysofnz.co.nz*. If you don't have a car, you must rely on the buses. *Intercity (intercity.co.nz)* has a comprehensive network across the entire country. The route Auckland–Wellington costs e.g. about NZ\$50.
For backpackers the Hop-on-Hop-off buses are ideal, as they can be used anytime and on repeated occasions. *Kiwi Experience (www.kiwiexperience. com)* and *Stray Travel (www.straytrav el.com)* offer reasonably priced tickets that can be used flexibly for different time intervals.
Two ferries operate between North- and South Island. In about 3.5 hours, either the *Bluebridge Ferry (www.blue bridge.co.nz)* or the *Interislander (www. greatjourneysofnz.co.nz)* takes you from Wellington to Picton. You can also reach islands like Stewart Island, Waiheke or Great Barrier Island by ferry.

TIME

If you travel a little further east from New Zealand, you cross the international date line and you start the day again (e.g. on the Cook Islands). However, there is a 13-hour time difference in New Zealand from GMT between the last Sunday in October and the last Sunday in March. Until the first Sunday in April the difference is then 12 hours. Afterwards, the time difference is 11 hours until the last Sunday in September; and until the last Sunday in October, the time gap is 12 hours again.
Information: *www.timeanddate.com*

TIPPING

In New Zealand it is not usual to leave a tip. When you leave the restaurant you pay at the bar.

ROAD ATLAS

The green line indicates the Discovery Tour "New Zealand at a glance"
The blue line indicates the other Discovery Tours

All tours are also marked on the pull-out map

Photo: Hiker on the Milford Track

Exploring New Zealand

The map on the back cover shows how
the area has been sub-divided

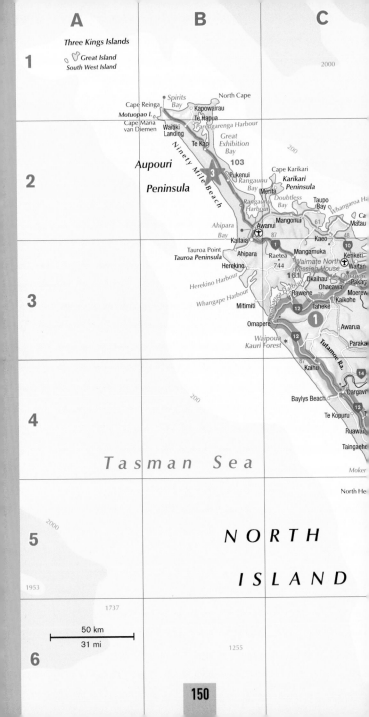

Three Kings Islands
Great Island
South West Island

2000

North Cape
Spirits Bay
Cape Reinga
Kapowairau
Motuopao I.
Te Hapua
Cape Maria van Diemen
Waitiki Landing
Parengarenga Harbour

Te Kao
Great Exhibition Bay

Aupouri
Ninety Mile Beach
103
Pukenui
Cape Karikari
Karikari Peninsula

Peninsula
Rangaunu Bay
Merita
Doubtless Bay
Taupo Bay
Whangaroa Ha

Rangaunu Harbour
Mangonui
61
Ca
Matau

Ahipara Bay
Awanui
87
Kaeo
48

Kaitaia
Mangamuka
10
Kerikeri
Tauroa Point
Ahipara
Raetea
Waimate North Mission House
Waitan
Tauroa Peninsula
744
16.1
Okaihau
Pakara
Herekino
Ohaeawai
Moerew

Herekino Harbour
Rawene
Taheke
Kaikohe

Whangape Harbour
Mitimiti
12
1
Awarua

Omapere
Parakai

Waipoua Kauri Forest
12

Tutamoe Ra.

Kaihu
14

87
Baylys Beach
Dargavi

Te Kopuru
12
T

Ruawai

Taingaehe

Moker

Tasman Sea

North He

NORTH

ISLAND

2000

1953

1737

50 km
31 mi

1255

150

PACIFIC OCEAN

Cape Brett

*Taupiri
Bay*
Home Point

Northland

*Whangaruru
Harbour*

va
a Bay
haka-
para

Whananaki

*Poor
Knights Is.*

Peninsula

Tutukaka

Ngunguru

Ngunguru Bay

Whangarei

Parua Bay

Whangarei Heads
Bream Head

Ruakaka

*Marotere Is.
Hen and
Chickens Is.*

aiotira

*Bream
Bay*

Waipu

Taranga I.

paroa

Brynderwyn

turoto

Mangawhai
Heads

Kaiwaka

*Little
Barrier I.*

Mt
Hauturu
722

Port Fitzroy

Rakitu I.

Great Barrier I.

Wellsford

158

Cape
Rodney

Leigh

Craddock Channel

Tryphena

Port
Albert

Tapora

Kaipara
Flats

Warkworth

Kawau I.

Cape Barrier

Cape Colville

Cuvier I.

RN

Puhoi
Tavern

Mahurangi

Mahurangi West

Waiwera

Port
Jackson

Port
Charles

*Great
Mercury I.*

*Red
Mercury I.*

arbour

each

Kaukapakapa

Helensville

Dairy
Flat

Orewa

Whangaparaoa

Albany

Whangaahei

Mercury Is.

Kuatonu

Mercury Bay

Coromandel

Kumeu

Rangitoto I.

*Haurakī
Gulf*

Waiheke I.

aimaiku

ai Beach

Waitakere

Blackpool

Howick

Onetangi

Coromandel

Ponui I.

Whitianga

Cooks Beach

Cathedral Cove

Hot Water Beach

UCKLAND

Huia

AKL

Papatoetoe

Maraetai

*Orere
Point*

Corogien

*Hot Water
Beach*

Tairua

The Aldermen Is.

Manurewa

Kohukohunui

Tapu

Pauanui

Peninsula

Matakawau

Papakura

688

*Firth
of
Thames*

103

25

Thames

Slipper I.

Clarks
Beach

Kaiaua

Waitaka-
ruru

Kopu

Pukekohe

Pokeno

16

Bombay

Ngatea

26

Whangamata

Waiuku

Waikato River

Port Waikato

Glen
Murray

22

125

Mangatarata

50

203

Paeroa

Mayor I.

25

Waihi

Waihi Beach

Coromandel Ra.

Naike

Te Kauwhata

*Lake
Waikare*

151

Tirohia

Aroha

152

Karewa I.

Waikorea

Huntly

Katikati

Matakana I.

200

2000

56

35

53

16

18

16

50

158

27

34

21

36

16

75

1

27

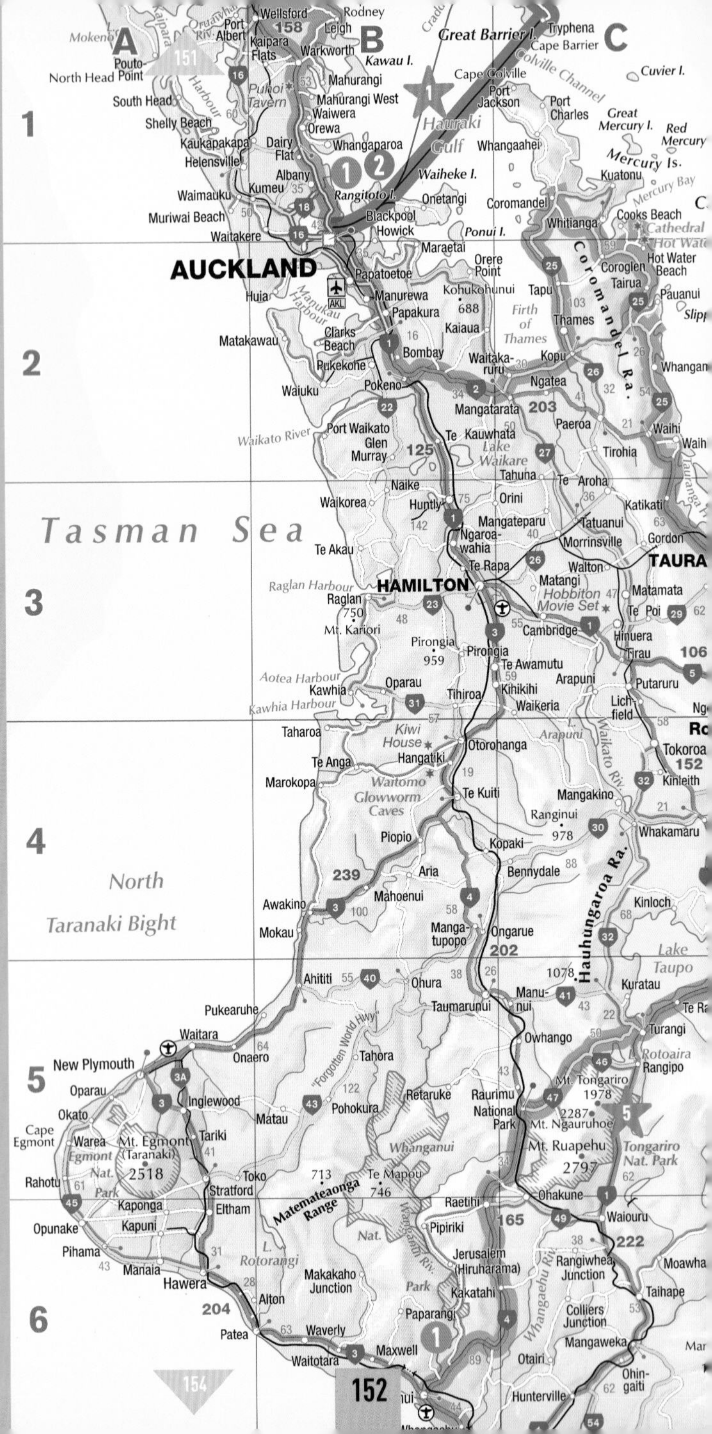
A
B
C
1
2
3
4
5
6
151
154
Wellsford
Rodney
158
Leigh
Port Albert
Kaipara Flats
Warkworth
Kawau I.
Great Barrier I.
Tryphena
Cape Barrier
Colville Channel
Cuvier I.
Mokeno
Pouto-Point
North Head
Kaipara Harbour
Puhoi Tavern
Mahurangi
Mahurangi West
Waiwera
Orewa
Whangaparoa
South Head
Shelly Beach
Kaukapakapa
Helensville
Dairy Flat
Albany
Kumeu
Waimauku
Muriwai Beach
Waitakere
Cape Colville
Port Jackson
Port Charles
Hauraki Gulf
Great Mercury I.
Red Mercury
Mercury Is.
Whangaahei
Waiheke I.
Rangitoto I.
Onetangi
Coromandel
Kuatonu
Mercury Bay
Blackpool
Howick
Ponui I.
Whitianga
Cooks Beach
Cathedral
Hot Water Beach
AUCKLAND
Maraetai
Orere Point
Papatoetoe
Huia
Manukau Harbour
AKL
Manurewa
Kohukohunui
688
Tapu
Coroglen
Tairua
Pauanui
Papakura
Firth of Thames
Thames
Coromandel Ra.
Matakawau
Clarks Beach
Kaiaua
Bombay
Pukekohe
Waitakaruru
Kopu
Whangamata
Waiuku
Pokeno
Ngatea
Mangatarata
203
Paeroa
Waihi
Waikato River
Port Waikato
Glen Murray
125
Te Kauwhata
Lake Waikare
Tirohia
Tahuna
Te Aroha
Naike
Waikorea
Huntly
Orini
Katikati
Tasman Sea
Mangateparu
Tatuanui
Te Akau
Ngaruawahia
Morrinsville
Gordon
TAURA
Te Rapa
Walton
Raglan Harbour
HAMILTON
Matangi
Hobbiton Movie Set
Matamata
Raglan
750
Mt. Kariori
Cambridge
Te Poi
Hinuera
Pirongia
959
Tirau
Te Awamutu
106
Aotea Harbour
Oparau
Arapuni
Putaruru
Kawhia
Tihiroa
Kihikihi
Kawhia Harbour
Waikeria
Lichfield
Taharoa
Kiwi House
Otorohanga
Tokoroa
152
Te Anga
Hangatiki
Waikato Riv.
Marokopa
Waitomo Glowworm Caves
Te Kuiti
Mangakino
Kinleith
Ranginui
978
Whakamaru
Piopio
Kopaki
Bennydale
Hauhungaroa Ra.
North Taranaki Bight
239
Aria
Awakino
Mahoenui
Kinloch
Mokau
Mangatupopo
Ongarue
202
Lake Taupo
Ahititi
Ohura
1078
Kuratau
Manunui
Pukearuhe
Taumarunui
Te Ra
Turangi
Waitara
Owhango
Rotoaira
New Plymouth
Onaero
Tahora
Rangipo
"Forgotten World Hwy"
Mt. Tongariro
1978
Oparau
Inglewood
Pohokura
Retaruke
Raurimu
2287
Okato
Matau
National Park
Mt. Ngauruhoe
Cape Egmont
Warea
Mt. Egmont (Taranaki)
Tariki
Whanganui
Mt. Ruapehu
Tongariro Nat. Park
Egmont Nat. Park
2518
2797
Rahotu
Toko
713
Te Mapou
746
Stratford
Matemateaonga Range
Ohakune
Kaponga
Eltham
Raetihi
Opunake
Kapuni
165
Waiouru
Pipiriki
Nat. Park
Whanganui Riv.
Pihama
L. Rotorangi
222
Manaia
Jerusalem (Hiruharama)
Rangiwhea Junction
Moawha
Hawera
Makakaho Junction
Whangaehu Riv.
Taihape
204
Alton
Kakatahi
Colliers Junction
Patea
Waverly
Paparangi
Mangaweka
Maxwell
Waitotara
Otairi
Ohingaiti
Hunterville

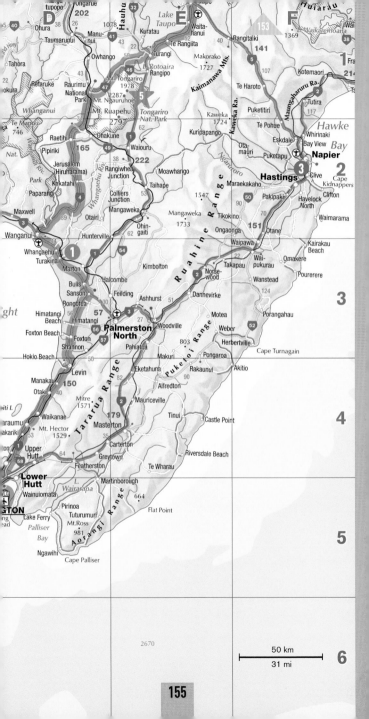

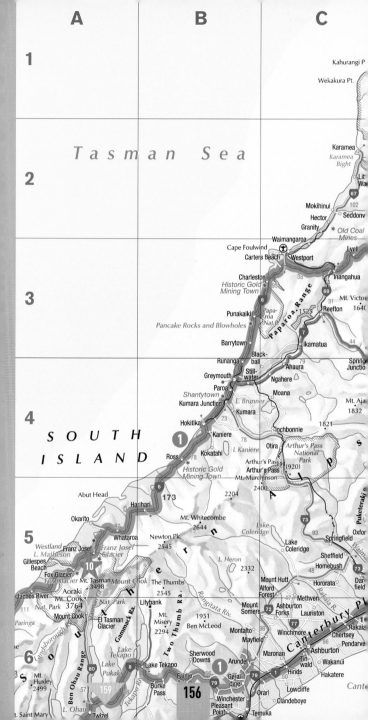

	A	B	C

1

Kahurangi P

Wekakura Pt.

2

T a s m a n S e a

Karamea
*Karamea
Bight*
Lit Wa
67
Mokihinui 102
Hector Seddonv
Granity
★ Old Coal
Waimangaroa Mines

3

Cape Foulwind ⚓ Lyell
Carters Beach Westport
Charleston 38 Inangahua
*Historic Gold
Mining Town* 95
6 Mt. Victo
Papa- 31 1640
roa 69
Nat. 152S Reefton
Punakaiki
Pancake Rocks and Blowholes ★ 7 44
Ikamatua
Barrytown Spring
Black- 79 Junctio
Runanga ball
Greymouth Stillwater Ahaura
Paroa Ngahere
Shantytown Moana
Kumara Junction L. Brunner Mt. Aja
1832

4

S O U T H   Hokitika Kumara
Kaniere 78 Inchbonnie 1821
ISLAND 23 Otira Arthur's Pass s
Ross L Kaniere National Park
78 Arthur's Pass P u
Historic Gold Arthur's Pass (920) e k
Mining Town Mt. Murchison t e
2400 A r
Abut Head 6 2204 a
173
Harihari n 73 Oxfor
Okarito Mt. Whitecombe 93 Springfield
Newton Pk. 2644 *Lake
Coleridge*

5

47 2545 t Lake Sheffield 73
Whataroa Coleridge Homebush
Westland Franz Josef h Darf
L. Matheson *Franz Josef* L. Heron
Gillespies *Glacier* e 2332 Mount Hutt
Beach 10 Alford
Fox Glacier Mt. Tasman r Forest Methven
Fox Glacier 3498 *Mount Cook* The Thumbs Hororata 47
Jacobs River Mt. Cook 2545 n Mount 72 Lauriston
Nat. Park 3764 Somers Forks
111 Mount Cook El Tasman Lilybank 1951 Montalto Winchmore Ashburton
Paringa Glacier Mt. Ben McLeod 36 Mayfield Wakanui
Misery Maronan Tin- Chertsey
2294 Two wald Pendarve

6

Mt. Huxley Ben Ohau Range 80 Lake Thumb Sherwood 1 Rakaia
2499 Tekapo Downs Arundel Hinds Hakatere
S 8 Lake Tekapo 79 Geraldine 79 1 Lowcliffe Cant
57 44 Fairlie 56 Winchester Orari Clandeboye
L. Ohau Twizel Burke **156** Pleasant Temuka
t. Saint Mary Lake Pass Point
Pukaki 159

Canterbury Pl
Canterbury Pl
Puketeraki

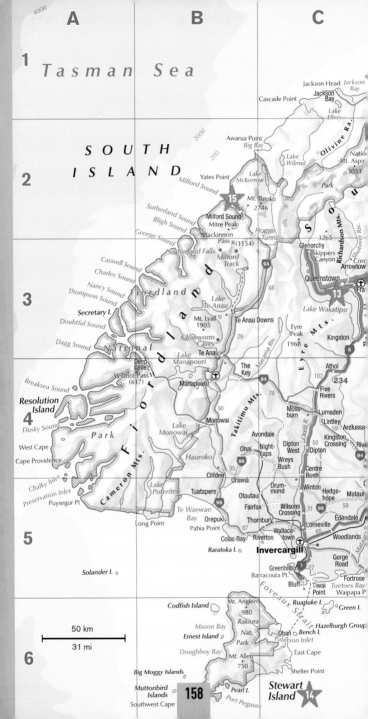

A

B

C

1

Tasman Sea

2

S O U T H

I S L A N D

4000

2000

200

Cascade Point

Jackson Head | Jackson Bay

Jackson Bay

Lake Ellery

Awarua Point
Big Bay

Yates Point

Milford Sound

Lake McKerrow

Lake Wilmot

Olivine Ra.

Natio
Mt. Aspir
3033

Park

Milford Sound
Mitre Peak

Mt. Tutoko
2746

Homer Tunnel

3265

Sutherland Sound

Bligh Sound

George Sound

Mackinnon
Pass (1154)

94

Glenorchy

Richardson Mts.

Shotover Rv.

Cor
Arrowtow

Caswell Sound

Sutherland Falls

Milford
Track

Skippers
Canyon

Queenstown

3

Charles Sound

Nancy Sound

Thompson Sound

Secretary I.

Doubtful Sound

Dagg Sound

Fiordland

Lake
Te Anau

Te Anau Downs

Mt. Lyall
1905

Te Anau

88

Eyre
Peak
1968

13

Fra

Lake Wakatipu

Kingston

National

Glowworm
Caves

Lake
Manapouri

29

Mararoa Rv.

Eyre Mts.

6

Athol

102

234

Deep
Cove

Wilmot Pass
(617)

Manapouri

The Key

94

78

4

Breaksea Sound

**Resolution
Island**

Dusky Sound

West Cape

Cape Providence

Park

Monowai

Lake
Monowai

Haurōko

Takitimu Mts.

90

Avondale

Ohai

Night-
caps

Dipton
West

Wreys
Bush

50

Mossburn

Lumsden

Lintley

59

Dipton

Centre
Bush

Ardlussa

Kingston
Crossing

Riv

94

Cameron Mts.

96

95

Clifden

Orawia

Drummond

Winton

Hedge-
hope

Matau

59

96

5

Chalky Inlet

Preservation Inlet

Puysegur Pt.

Lake
Poteriteri

Tuatapere

Otautau

Fairfax

Wilsons
Crossing

Edendale

99

Te Waewae
Bay

Orepuki

Thornbury,

31

Long Point

Pahia Point

Colac Bay

87

Riverton

Wallace-
town

65

Lorneville

Woodlands

Invercargill

1

27

Gorge
Road

Raratoka I.

Greenhills

Barracouta Pt.

Bluff

Tiwai
Point

Fortrose

Mataū

Toetoes Bay
Waipapa P

Solander I. ○

6

50 km

31 mi

Codfish Island

Mt. Anglem
980

Rakiura

Mason Bay

Ernest Island ○

*Nat.
Park*

Doughboy Bay

Mt. Allen
750

Big Moggy Islands

**Muttonbird
Islands**

Southwest Cape

Pearl I.

Port Pegasus

Foveaux Strait

Ruapuke I.

Bench I. ○

Green I. ○

Oban

Hazelburgh Group

Paterson Inlet

East Cape

Shelter Point

**Stewart
Island**

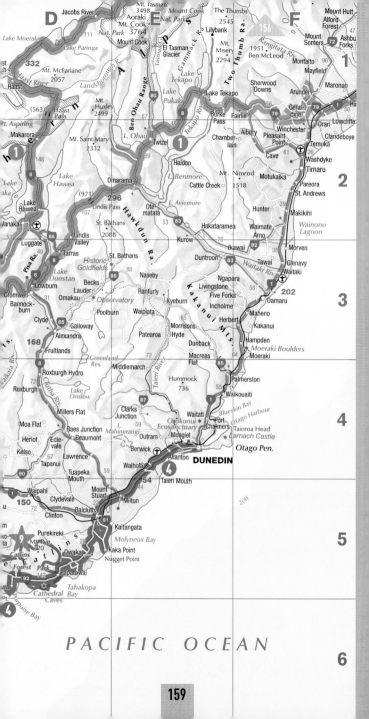

PACIFIC OCEAN

KEY TO ROAD ATLAS

Autobahn, mehrspurige Straße - in Bau Highway, multilane divided road - under construction	════ ═ ═ ═	Autoroute, route à plusieurs voies - en construction Autosnelweg, weg met meer rijstroken - in aanleg
Fernverkehrsstraße - in Bau Trunk road - under construction	──── ─ ─ ─	Route à grande circulation - en construction Weg voor interlokaal verkeer - in aanleg
Hauptstraße Principal highway		Route principale Hoofdweg
Nebenstraße Secondary road		Route secondaire Overige verharde wegen
Fahrweg, Piste Practicable road, track		Chemin carrossable, piste Weg, piste
Straßennummerierung Road numbering	E20 11 70 26 5 40 9	Numérotage des routes Wegnummering
Entfernungen in Kilometer Distances in kilometers	259 130 129	Distances en kilomètres Afstand in kilometers
Höhe in Meter - Pass Height in meters - Pass	1365 •	Altitude en mètres - Col Hoogte in meters - Pas
Eisenbahn - Eisenbahnfähre Railway - Railway ferry	──── ·········	Chemin de fer - Ferry-boat Spoorweg - Spoorpont
Autofähre - Schifffahrtslinie Car ferry - Shipping route		Bac autos - Ligne maritime Autoveer - Scheepvaartlijn
Wichtiger internationaler Flughafen - Flughafen Major international airport - Airport	✈ ✈	Aéroport importante international - Aéroport Belangrijke internationale luchthaven - Luchthaven
Internationale Grenze - Provinzgrenze International boundary - Province boundary		Frontière internationale - Limite de Province Internationale grens - Provinciale grens
Unbestimmte Grenze Undefined boundary		Frontière d'Etat non définie Rijksgrens onbepaalt
Zeitzonengrenze Time zone boundary	-4h Greenwich Time -3h Greenwich Time	Limite de fuseau horaire Tijdzone-grens
Hauptstadt eines souveränen Staates National capital	**MANILA**	Capitale nationale Hoofdstad van een souvereine staat
Hauptstadt eines Bundesstaates Federal capital	**Kuching**	Capitale d'un état fédéral Hoofdstad van een deelstaat
Sperrgebiet Restricted area		Zone interdite Verboden gebied
Nationalpark National park		Parc national Nationaal park
Antikes Baudenkmal Ancient monument	∴	Monument antiques Antiek monument
Sehenswertes Kulturdenkmal Interesting cultural monument	★ Angkor Wat	Monument culturel interéssant Bezienswaardig cultuurmonument
Sehenswertes Naturdenkmal Interesting natural monument	★ Ha Long Bay	Monument naturel interéssant Bezienswaardig natuurmonument
Brunnen Well	‿	Puits Bron
MARCO POLO Erlebnistour 1 MARCO POLO Discovery Tour 1		MARCO POLO Tour d'aventure 1 MARCO POLO Avontuurlijke Routes 1
MARCO POLO Erlebnistouren MARCO POLO Discovery Tours		MARCO POLO Tours d'aventure MARCO POLO Avontuurlijke Routes
MARCO POLO Highlight	★1	MARCO POLO Highlight

MARCO POLO TRAVEL GUIDES

Algarve
Amsterdam
Andalucia
Athens
Australia
Austria
Bali & Lombok
Bangkok
Barcelona
Berlin
Brazil
Bruges
Brussels
Budapest
Bulgaria
California
Cambodia
Canada East
Canada West / Rockies
& Vancouver
Cape Town &
Garden Route
Cape Verde
Channel Islands
Chicago & The Lakes
China
Cologne
Copenhagen
Corfu
Costa Blanca
& Valencia
Costa Brava
Costa del Sol &
Granada
Costa Rica
Crete
Cuba
Cyprus (North and
South)
Devon & Cornwall
Dresden
Dubai

Dublin
Dubrovnik &
Dalmatian Coast
Edinburgh
Egypt
Egypt Red Sea Resorts
Finland
Florence
Florida
French Atlantic Coast
French Riviera
(Nice, Cannes & Monaco)
Fuerteventura
Gran Canaria
Greece
Hamburg
Hong Kong & Macau
Ibiza
Iceland
India
India South
Ireland
Israel
Istanbul
Italy
Japan
Jordan
Kos
Krakow
Lake District
Lake Garda
Lanzarote
Las Vegas
Lisbon
London
Los Angeles
Madeira & Porto Santo
Madrid
Maldives
Mallorca
Malta & Gozo
Mauritius

Menorca
Milan
Montenegro
Morocco
Munich
Naples & Amalfi Coast
New York
New Zealand
Norway
Oslo
Oxford
Paris
Peru & Bolivia
Phuket
Portugal
Prague
Rhodes
Rome
Salzburg
San Francisco
Santorini
Sardinia
Scotland
Seychelles
Shanghai
Sicily
Singapore
South Africa
Sri Lanka
Stockholm
Switzerland
Tenerife
Thailand
Tokyo
Turkey
Turkey South Coast
Tuscany
United Arab Emirates
USA Southwest
(Las Vegas, Colorado,
New Mexico, Arizona
& Utah)
Venice
Vienna
Vietnam
Zakynthos & Ithaca,
Kefalonia, Lefkas

Travel with
Insider
Tips

INDEX

This index lists all sights and destinations featured in this guide. Numbers in bold indicate a main entry.